Keith Ward is an Anglican priest and was a Canon of Christ Church, Oxford. He has been F. D. Maurice Professor of Moral Theology in the University of London, Professor of the History and Philosophy of Religion at the University of London, Professor of Divinity at Gresham College, London, and Regius Professor of Divinity at the University of Oxford. He is a Fellow of the British Academy and the author of *What the Bible Really Teaches: A Challenge for Fundamentalists* (SPCK, 2004). SPCK also published *Comparative Theology: Essays for Keith Ward*, edited by T. W. Bartel, in 2003.

CHRISTIANITY

A Guide for the Perplexed

Keith Ward

First published in Great Britain in 2007

Society for Promoting Christian Knowledge
36 Causton Street
London SW1P 4ST

British Library Cataloguing-in-Publication Data
A catalogue record for this book is available from the British Library

ISBN: 978-0-281-05896-9

1 3 5 7 9 10 8 6 4 2

Typeset by Graphicraft Ltd, Hong Kong
Printed in Great Britain by Bookmarque Ltd

Contents

Preface

I wrote this book for three main reasons. First, I wanted to set out as briefly as possible a form of Christian faith that takes full account of modern science and of the best biblical scholarship. Christian teaching often seems to be presented in a way that is irrelevant to, or even in opposition to, modern knowledge and to the sort of study of the Bible that takes place in most universities. I want to show how Christian faith can provide a spiritual teaching that is fully consistent with the best modern knowledge, and that gives a moral and spiritual depth to such knowledge that might otherwise be lacking.

So, for example, I do not start with the story of Adam and Eve in a garden – a starting point that can easily create problems when set alongside modern cosmology. I start with an outline of cosmic history from the Big Bang. I do not assume that the Bible is a specially inspired book. I seek to place it in the context of the global development of religions in early human history. I try to set out Christian faith as an intellectually and spiritually profound teaching. This is, of course, only one possible form of Christian faith, and I make no claim to have discovered the 'true essence' of Christianity. But it is a form of spiritual belief and practice that seems to me particularly well suited to the scientific and critical age in which we live, and it is written for those who wish both to accept the best scientific, historical and philosophical thought that the modern world has to offer, and to discover an intellectually satisfying and morally inspiring spiritual path to follow.

Second, I wanted to provide a short introduction to some of the great writers in Christian history, and provide a short systematic outline of the best historical and contemporary thinking about Christian faith. So I try to cover the main doctrines of Christianity (creation, incarnation, the atonement, the Trinity and eternal life), what major theologians have said about them, and how I would interpret them today.

Third, I wrote each chapter as a meditation on some aspect of Christian thought. Writing it has been a sort of spiritual exercise, and for me the ideal way of reading it would be to take one chapter a day, and use it as a starting point for prayer and reflection. It is meant to be, if this is not too grandiose a thought, a kind of prayer as well as an intellectual exercise.

Introduction

The text is divided into eight parts. The first is an exposition of the modern scientific view of the origin of the cosmos and the development of human life, seen from a religious viewpoint.

The second part discusses the Hebrew Bible as a record of the development of religious thought in one ancient tradition.

In the third part, I examine the way in which Christians see Jesus as a fulfilment of this Hebrew prophetic tradition. I ask what we can reliably say about Jesus in the light of modern critical study of the Bible, and I show how a properly critical study can deepen faith in Jesus as saviour of the world.

The fourth part outlines the way in which the major Christian doctrines of the incarnation, the Trinity, the atonement and the Church developed in the early Christian world, and suggests contemporary ways of interpreting these doctrines.

Fifth, I examine the development of other religious traditions – particularly the Indian and East Asian – so that the Christian tradition can be placed within the stream of developing religious life throughout the world. I am particularly interested in the way in which the diverse traditions can positively interact with one another to provide a wider and deeper understanding of God's purpose for humanity.

The sixth part considers a number of important movements in the history of Christian thought – early Eastern Orthodox theology, medieval Latin thought, the Reformation, the European Enlightenment, German liberalism, and the growth of liberation theologies – to show some of the many varieties of Christian belief, and how they have developed historically in diverse cultures.

In the seventh part I turn to the future, both the possible future for Christianity on earth, and the ultimate future of humanity in the resurrection of the dead and the creation of a 'new heaven and earth'.

Finally, the eighth part suggests six paths of prayer, as an introduction to some practical ways of making Christian faith a real and transforming influence on daily life. The sort of Christian faith I expound in this book may be called a liberal Christian faith. But for some people the word 'liberal' suggests a faith without definite content or strong moral commitment. This part is meant to outline a spirituality and personal commitment that is strong and firmly centred on the revelation of God in the person of Jesus, and that makes a decisive difference to everyday living.

The Creation

1
The beginning

In the beginning of this universe, there was no space and no time. There were no planets or stars. There was nothing made of matter at all.

Then, about 14 thousand million years ago, God created matter, space and time. From a tiny region of unimaginable heat and density – over 100 thousand million degrees Celsius, and four thousand million times denser than water – space began to expand at enormous speed. In a vast explosion of energy, millions of tiny particles – electrons, positrons, neutrinos and photons – scintillated in and out of existence in a huge explosion of dazzling light.

Rapidly cooling and expanding, after a few hundred thousand years, some of these tiny particles bonded together into the simplest atoms, hydrogen and helium, and these condensed to form the gaseous clouds that were to become the galaxies and stars.

There are over 100 million galaxies in the universe that we can observe from our planet, earth, and our own galaxy, the Milky Way, is just one of them. There are over 100 million stars in a typical galaxy, and our star, the sun, is just one of them. We have been able to see galaxies about ten thousand million light years away, and we and they are still moving apart at about three-fifths of the speed of light.

Light travels at 186,000 miles per second. It travels from the sun to the earth – a distance of 93 million miles – in about eight minutes. Light takes ten thousand million years to travel from some of the furthest galaxies we can see. They are far away and still receding, as this universe continues its expansion from the moment of its explosive origin.

The vastness of space dwarfs human imagination. But our whole universe is perhaps only a tiny part of other and vastly greater forms of space and time. And they are all little more than the blink of an eye before the infinity of God, who is beyond every space and time, who originates and sustains them all, however many there may be. All these worlds of time and space are brought to be, and held in being, solely by the power of God, who sets the laws of their development and the pattern of their fundamental forms. The galaxies and stars declare the awe-inspiring power, wonder, beauty and wisdom of God. As the Psalmist put it, 'The heavens are telling the glory of God; and the firmament proclaims his handiwork' (Psalm 19.1).

2
The wisdom of creation

Stars are condensations of galactic dust. Within the intense nuclear fusion of their interiors, heavier elements are constructed. Among those elements is carbon, the basis of all life-forms that we know. Many, probably many billions, of stars are circled by planets, and our planet is propitiously placed for the development of life. The conditions needed for the development of life are very specifically balanced. The initial asymmetry of the universe, and the rate of its expansion, need to be exactly what they are – even to the ninth decimal place – to enable galaxies and stars to form. The fundamental forces of nature – gravity, electromagnetism, and the nuclear forces – need to be exactly balanced to enable stable atoms to come into being. If the nuclear force that binds protons and neutrons together was changed by more than 1 or 2 per cent, carbon atoms would not form. The properties of those atoms need to be exactly correlated to enable complex molecules to endure and replicate. Earth needs to be just at the right distance from its star, the sun, to enable carbon molecules to develop into proteins and nucleic acids. Oxygen and nitrogen in the atmosphere have to be correctly balanced, atmospheric protection from harmful radiation must be provided, and something like large outer planets, such as Jupiter, must exist to deflect many potentially destructive asteroids. The development of life from the basic constituents of the material universe shows a breathtaking balance and integration in the fundamental structure and laws of nature, and in the ordering of its cosmic unfolding. The universe is ordered towards the existence of life, though whether that is only on this planet or also on others we do not yet know.

Life on earth unfolds by processes of increasing complexity and integration, successively building more and more complex structures on relatively simple foundations. Yet even that simplicity shows pattern and correlation. In 1953 the structure of DNA was discovered, and we now know the incredible arrangement of the four chemical bases along the intertwined strands of DNA that makes up a code that contains instructions for building proteins into organic cells. These cells, all initially identical, diversify as bodies grow, so that they form different organs – liver, heart, lungs, limbs and eyes. The DNA code replicates itself in each generation, but it modifies itself with each replication in such a way that great organic diversity is generated, and over time some life-forms change to become more adapted to their environment.

Over thousands of generations, organic life has evolved from simple one-celled organisms to the complex bodies we see on earth today, containing millions of cells working together to sustain highly complex organisms. Single-celled life-forms began to exist on earth about four thousand million years ago. Multi-celled life first existed in the sea, then over millions of years it developed into varied forms of plant and animal life on land. On this planet, millions of forms of organism gradually adapted more closely to the conditions in which they lived, and the ecosystem of the earth became a rich and interconnected web of growing, reproducing and changing organisms. Central nervous systems and sense organs evolved, so that animals could increasingly sense and respond to their environment, and move around to find new forms of food. The earth was filled with a surging panoply of beautiful, fantastic, creative and responsive life, utilizing the basic energies of the cosmos to grow, develop, and explore every possibility for flourishing that this small blue world offered.

The creation story in the first chapter of Genesis is not meant to be a literal scientific account, in the modern sense. It is a poem to express the truth that everything in the universe is created solely by God. Nevertheless, it shows great insight in thinking of the process of creation as divided into periods of time ('days'), in which light, the stars, plants, sea creatures and animals successively came into existence. The most important thing it says is that 'God saw that it was good' (Genesis 1.25). The elegance and order, the precise balance and adjustment, the creativity and complexity of life, are indeed beautiful and desirable. We can share in appreciating and desiring that beauty, like the Lady Wisdom in the book of Proverbs, who says, speaking of the creation of the world: 'then I was beside him [God], like a little child; and I was daily his delight, rejoicing before him always, rejoicing in his inhabited world' (Proverbs 8.30–31).

3
The polarity of being

The universe began with an explosion of light. The first particles of matter flashed in and out of existence, scintillating, colliding, decaying and vanishing in shimmering patterns of evanescent energy. The first stars were furnaces of raging fire, and as they destroyed themselves in bursts of searing flame, they forged new and complex elements, seeding the early universe with future life.

So from the beginning conflict and destruction, transience and decay, were inseparable from the creation of harmony and new life. Out of the death of atoms and the destruction of their primal energies emerged new and higher forms of life and complexity. The beauty of the stars flows from their self-conflagration, and the glory of the galaxies is part of the story of their inevitable decay towards the long, slow, frozen emptiness at the end of time.

This pattern of polarity, conflict, emergent complexity, decay and death is repeated in the evolutionary story of life on earth. For each adaptive mutation, there are many that are harmful and destructive. Each form of organic life survives by the consumption of energy. Life preys on life, and we live only by the destruction of life, as it becomes our food.

Humans have become the dominant species on earth only by destroying or subjugating their competitors. Lust – the desire to propagate more successfully than others – and aggression – the desire to win the struggle for survival in a world of scarce resources – are natural and genetically inbred in any dominant species. Thus death and the capacity for destruction lie in the human world from the beginning, as well as creative life and the capacity for goodness.

This universe is both terrible and beautiful – terrifying in destructive power, beautiful and elegant in its fragile harmony and complexity. God creates for the sake of goodness, but that cannot be attained in this universe without the terrors of destruction and suffering, for such things are built into the structure of the cosmos. To understand fully the laws of the cosmos, and the distinctive goods it makes possible, would be to understand the necessity of conflict, destruction, suffering and death.

God will seek to limit destruction, and will, the Christian gospel affirms, finally overcome it. But some degree of polarity and conflict is unavoidable in any emergent and dynamically creative material universe that is grounded in, exists in relative independence from, but is drawn through striving and gradual development towards final reunion with, supreme Spirit.

The Bible speaks cryptically of these things, in passages often overlooked in accounts of the creation. The first chapter of Genesis speaks of 'the great deep' (*tohu-wa-bohu*), covered by darkness, swept by the winds of God. In that great deep, the sea of primeval chaos, dwells Leviathan, also called Rahab, the mighty dragon of the deep, of whom the Psalmist says, 'You [LORD God] rule the raging of the sea; when its waves rise, you still them. You crushed Rahab like a carcass' (Psalm 89.9–10). The same thought occurs in Psalm 74: 'you broke the heads of the dragons in the waters. You crushed the heads of Leviathan' (Psalm 74.13–14). Job speaks of '[God], who alone stretched out the heavens and trampled the back of the sea dragon' (Job 9.8), and Isaiah rhetorically asks,

'Was it not you who cut Rahab in pieces, who pierced the dragon?' (Isaiah 51.9).

In the image of the dragon Leviathan there is an echo of the Babylonian dragon Tiamat, the monster of chaos and the sea, who was killed by the god Marduk, god of order and the city. In the Babylonian story, many gods arise from primordial chaos, and out of their warfare the world is born. The Bible transforms the story, while leaving it still recognizable. There is only one creator god, from whom all things arise. But in forming heaven and earth that god must have 'stilled the Sea' (Job 26.12) and 'pierced the fleeing serpent' (Job 26.13). Chaos and darkness exist as well as order and light. At present the serpent is contained but not yet destroyed. But at the end of time, 'the LORD with his cruel and great and strong sword will punish Leviathan the fleeing serpent, Leviathan the twisting serpent, and he will kill the dragon that is in the sea' (Isaiah 27.1). So in the final vision of the New Jerusalem the writer says, 'the sea was no more' (Revelation 21.1). Chaos and night have been finally overcome.

These are strange mythological images, but they show awareness that conflict and struggle are essential to the structure of this universe. God's purpose in creation is good, but it cannot exist without the conflict that generates creative emergence. The modern scientific view of the history of the universe helps to show how this is so.

4
The image of God

Between five and ten million years ago, the first humans evolved from a common ancestor that we share with our closest genetic relatives, the chimpanzees. Humans are genetically very close to the higher primates, sharing 99.4 per cent of the genetic code of chimpanzees. Yet humans are quite distinctive. According to the book of Genesis, God said, 'Let us make humankind in our image, according to our likeness' (Genesis 1.26).

To be made in the image of God is to reflect in a very limited but real way some of the main attributes of God. God has complete understanding of all things, knowing everything in the deepest and most intimate way, envisaging all that is possible and perfectly remembering all that has been actual. So humans have the capacity to understand the nature of the universe, to envisage possibilities for the future, recall and learn from what has happened to them, and achieve an abstract intellectual knowledge of the mathematical beauty of being.

God is the supreme creator of all, bringing into being innumerable objects and states in joyful freedom. So humans have a power of creativity, able to bring things into being for the sake of their goodness and beauty, and realizing their own potential by free creative activity.

God appreciates and delights in all the good things of creation, is compassionate to those creatures who suffer, and actively strives for their happiness and welfare. So humans are able to appreciate beauty and goodness for its own sake, to show kindness and compassion to those in trouble, and to act on universal principles of justice and morality.

Humans are distinguished among animals on earth by their capacity for intellectual understanding, free creativity, and responsible action. This is what makes them persons, capable of relating to other persons and to God as free, co-operating subjects of intellectually comprehended experience and morally responsible action. This is what traditional Christian theologians meant by saying that humans have intellectual souls.

Any creature with these capacities, regardless of its species, is a person, able to be aware of its own continuing existence as a responsible agent and subject of experience. There may be millions of different species of persons in the universe – we do not know. But on earth *homo sapiens* is the only known biological species fully to possess and exercise these capacities – a distinctiveness that is expressed by the human use of sophisticated forms of language.

Persons have a special moral dignity, because they are responsible moral subjects with an awareness of their continuing existence through time. As spiritual subjects, they are capable of conscious relationship with God, and have the possibility of continuing to exist as subjects even after the dissolution of their physical bodies. In traditional language, human souls are potentially immortal. As humans are made in the image of God, so their proper destiny is that they should find their fulfilment in God, when likeness can be transformed into union, and image and original can be made one.

5
The Fall

Human beings carry with them the capacities for competition and aggression that helped them to become the dominant species on earth. But they also carry the potential for understanding, creativity and co-operation that gives them their distinctive nature as persons. Millions of years ago, as responsible agency began to develop in the human or proto-human species, a basic moral choice began to emerge, a choice between the egoistic drive for dominance and power and the possibility of acting for the sake of good alone. However restricted and fitful that choice was, it seems reasonable to think that God, who is Supreme

Goodness, would have been a spiritual presence able to illuminate and empower actions for good, actions that would enable human persons to draw nearer to fuller knowledge of God, and desire closer relationship with God. The subsequent course of human history shows that in the earliest stages of human existence, choices were made for power and self-interest. We do not know how long it took, but eventually such choices had the effect of corrupting the whole of human society.

Early Catholic theologians, who had no knowledge of evolution, spoke of 'original sin' as the loss of sanctifying grace, which deprived humans of a strong sense of the presence of God and of the ability to do good easily. We can see how continued choices against the good, over generations, would mean that children were brought up in societies in which it was no longer easy and natural to do good, and in which a sense of God had been dimmed by repeated turning from the light of goodness.

In today's world we inherit a nature with the same genetic ambiguity as our earliest human ancestors. But we are 'born in sin', in that our society lacks a clear knowledge of God, and teaches that it is natural to put our own interests first. So the human will is weakened and inclined to evil simply by being formed in such a society. Humans are estranged from God, seeing God as a tyrant to be propitiated or evaded. They are estranged from the world, regarding it as something to be used simply for human purposes, and not valued as a divine creation. They are estranged from their fellows, seeing them as threats and enemies. And they are estranged from themselves, from what makes them distinctively persons, the capacity for responsible creative understanding and goodness, which is suppressed by the power of self-centred passion and desire.

The human world has become a world of sin and death – a world corrupted by our inability to know what is good and to do what is good, and in which the desires that control human lives lead to frustration, despair, and the spiritual death of a life cut off from God, who is the only source of true life, joy and human fulfilment.

It is in this sense that 'the wages of sin is death' (Romans 6.23). It is not that God will kill us for some isolated act of disobedience – a harsh punishment for a minor offence. It is that we die to our true selves, to the joy and friendship that God wills for us, to the promise of fulfilment that human life holds, by becoming enslaved to selfish desires, which promise much but deliver only emptiness, disillusion, and finally the disintegration and death of the true self.

The Genesis story of 'the Fall' (Genesis 3) is a symbolic account of how humankind (Adam and Eve) followed the destructive possibilities inherent in their natures (the serpent), and grasped at knowledge (the forbidden fruit) without responsibility, for the sake of power rather than of goodness. The consequence was all the suffering that people bring on others and on themselves (ejection from the Garden of Bliss), as they follow the paths of selfish desire that lead to death. An evolutionary account of human origins helps to give new depth and plausibility to this ancient story of the moral failure of the human race.

The Hebrew Bible

6
The birth of monotheism

For thousands of millennia humans lived as hunter–gatherers, bonded together in groups for protection and survival, yet divided from one another by hatred, greed and ignorance. The God from whom they had turned away was known by them only as a remote spiritual presence, or in the form of the powers of the natural world, animal and elemental, that bounded and circumscribed their lives. But God was not absent. In the gift of animal and plant life, in the dark mysteries of the cave, and in the felt unity of one life within all things, there was a sense of spiritual gift and presence. In each generation, shamans or seers arose who were mediators between the world of spirits and the world of humans, bringing guidance and healing to their fellows. In dreams and visions they kept alive a hope of future purpose and future good towards which the spirits were leading them.

In a land between high mountains, the desert and the sea, almost four thousand years ago, these early forms of spiritual faith began to develop in a way that was to change the whole world. A group of nomadic desert tribes, tracing their ancestry to Abraham, came to believe that there was just one God, creator of all things in heaven and earth, who called them to exclusive loyalty to God as their protector.

This was a long and gradual development, and the Hebrew Bible is one of the best records we have of the origins of monotheism, belief in one creator God. Many traces of early polytheism remain. Psalm 95 states, 'The LORD is a great God, and a great King above all gods' (Psalm 95.3). When Solomon builds the Temple, he says, 'The house that I am about to build will be great, for our God is greater than other gods' (2 Chronicles 2.5). Psalm 82 says, 'God has taken his place in the divine council; in the midst of the gods he holds judgement' (Psalm 82.1).

Such quotations remind us of a time when the God of Abraham was thought to be one of many gods or divine spirits, though he was naturally thought of as the greatest of the gods. The God of Israel is the god who protects the children of Abraham, but other nations have their own gods: 'For all the peoples walk, each in the name of its god, but we will walk in the name of the LORD our God' (Micah 4.5).

However, by the time chapters 40—55 of the book of Isaiah (sometimes called 'second Isaiah' or 'deutero-Isaiah') were written, in the sixth century BC, the prophets, successors of the seers of the ancient Hebrew tribes, were able to say unequivocally that 'I am God, and there is no other' (Isaiah 45.22). All other gods are now regarded as idols, as non-existent, and the God of Israel is the one and only creator of all things.

In the Hebrew Bible we can see a development from what was perhaps in early times the idea of a tribal war-god (the 'Lord of Hosts', though this was later interpreted as Lord of all the hosts of heaven) to the idea of one sole creator of the whole universe. Corresponding to this development, the idea of a 'seer', a provider of oracles, became that of a 'prophet' (cf. 1 Samuel 9.9), one who has insight into the will of the creator, and realizes that the creator calls for uncompromising commitment to justice and *chesed* (the Hebrew word for loving-kindness): 'Let justice roll down like waters, and righteousness like an ever-flowing stream' (Amos 5.24). At that point a spirituality of commerce with the spirits to avoid harm and gain good fortune is transformed into a spirituality of devotion to the moral purpose of the one and only creator God. Among the descendants of Abraham, ethical monotheism was born.

7
The Law of Moses

The Hebrew Bible (which Christians call the Old Testament) is a collection of 'books', written, collected and edited over many years, generally accepted by Jews and Christians as an authoritative account of early Jewish history and belief. The first five books, the Pentateuch, comprise the written Torah, or Law, traditionally thought of as given by God to the prophet Moses. For Jews, the Mishnah, or 'Instruction', is equally important, as the oral law given to Moses. It was collected in written form in the third century AD, and forms part of the Talmud, which contains laws on many topics, together with commentaries on them.

According to tradition there are 613 commandments in the Law, ranging from general moral principles like 'Love your neighbour as yourself' (Leviticus 19.18) to rules for ritually pure food like 'You shall not eat anything with its blood' (Leviticus 19.26). There are laws for ritual purity and religious festivals and sacrifices, for agriculture and the conduct of war, for crime and punishment, for the family and property, and for just and merciful conduct. For observant Jews, the Law sets out the way of life that God commands. It is a joy and privilege to keep the Law, for God revealed it to Moses as the true way to human well-being, and to keep the Law is to live under the guidance and protection of God.

What is distinctive about the God of Moses is that God reveals through the prophet the way in which humans are to live. Jesus, as an observant Jew, took the Law very seriously. According to Matthew, he said, 'Until heaven and earth pass away, not one letter, not one stroke of a letter, will pass from the law until all is accomplished' (Matthew 5.18). At the same time, Jesus saw that the two great commandments, in the light of which all others are to be interpreted, are to love God with all your heart and to love your neighbour as yourself (Matthew 22.36–40).

Keeping the Law is not a matter of blind obedience to a set of arbitrary rules. It is a matter of seeing what love of God and of your fellow-humans requires. For Jews, it may require keeping specific food and ritual laws just because God commands them. The purpose of such laws is to set Jews apart, as a people devoted to God in a special way. But it is important to see that for Jews the Law is a living, developing body of principles. The written laws often provide specific rules for particular times and places. Lawyers (the rabbis) have to discern the principles underlying such laws, and see how such principles might apply in very different circumstances. This is a complex process that allows argument and disagreement. The Law is not inhumane or inflexible. It points to the need to discern God's will for human fulfilment in very different times and places. It needs to be interpreted with love and concern for human welfare. And it insists that true religion requires a passion for justice, a concern for the oppressed, and a commitment to shape the world in accordance with God's will that goodness should flourish.

Most modern Christian scholars would see the Law not as literally given to Moses by God, but as codifying insights built up over many generations, as prophets and legislators gradually tried to discern God's will for their people. But the figure of Moses stands for a firm belief that God had called the people of the twelve tribes into a special relationship, which required of them a commitment to love the creator and the world and all the people God had created. The belief that God loved the created world, and called human persons to share in that love, was a profoundly new religious insight. The special vocation of the Hebrew tribes was to proclaim that insight to the whole inhabited earth.

8

The prophets

The Torah is not just a set of abstract commandments. It arises out of the history of the twelve tribes, and their developing discernment of the character and purpose of God. The Hebrew Bible relates that history. It tells how Abraham journeyed from Ur to the land of Canaan and had a vision in which God made a covenant with Abraham that he would be the ancestor of a great people who would live at peace in Canaan, and be a means of blessing for all the earth, as long as the children of Abraham obeyed God's Law.

It tells how the Hebrews became slaves in Egypt, and were liberated from slavery by mighty acts of God. They wandered in the wilderness for 40 years, led by the warrior-prophet Moses. Under Joshua (the name means 'God saves') they conquered Canaan, and eventually established a monarchy, celebrating King David as the founder of a great dynasty that would never perish.

Yet within a hundred years the kingdom was divided, ten tribes forming Israel in the north and the rump forming Judah in the south. The Bible has little that is good to say about the northern kings. Israel fell to the Assyrians in 721 BC, the people were sent into exile, and Israel ceased to exist. Judah survived a little longer, but it too was conquered, this time by the Babylonians. Jerusalem, the capital of Judah, was destroyed, and most of the population were deported to Babylon.

The biblical history ends with the return of many of the exiles, the rebuilding of the Temple in Jerusalem, and the rediscovery of the Law. Once again there was hope for a better future. But once again that hope was to be dashed, as the land was ruled by various great powers, and by the time of Jesus the kings of Palestine were little more than puppets of the Roman Empire. The Jerusalem Temple was destroyed in AD 70 by the Romans, who finally eliminated even the name of Jerusalem and banned all Jews from the area in AD 135. It seemed that the promise to Abraham had at last come to an end.

Most biblical scholars think that parts of the Bible, especially the court records of the monarchy, provide some of the most reliable ancient history we have. But much of the very earliest Jewish history is reconstructed much later, perhaps even after the return from exile in Babylon, and it incorporates different interpretations of Jewish history. In its final edited form, the biblical history provides a theological interpretation of history, which tries to show how what happens is the result of obedience to or rejection of God and the Law.

That history is a tragic one, for both kings and people repeatedly reject the prophets and give way to greed and injustice. So they break the covenant God had made with them, and God's judgement is that their destructive actions bring destruction on themselves. Yet time and again God walks with them in their distress, holds out the hope of forgiveness and return, liberates them from oppression, and makes possible a new start.

Even the final exile from Jerusalem was not the end, for as Jews spread throughout the world in the diaspora, there were those who remained faithful to the ancient covenant, and God did not forget them. In 1948 Israel was created, though as a secular state, and religious Jews are still seeking to discover its proper role in the history of God's relationship with humanity. Part of that role was to give the world knowledge of one creator God of justice and loving-kindness. Whatever that role now is, the history of Israel is a testimony to the severity of God's judgement, the breadth of God's forgiveness, the power of God's liberation and the never-failing possibility of God's renewal.

Human history in general is a tragic one, for humans are still locked into the greed, hatred and violence that has marked their existence throughout recorded time. But, however partially and fitfully, God has spoken through the prophets of Israel and Judah, revealing the divine will to liberate from evil and reunite human lives to the divine life. The biblical history of the Hebrews expresses the complex interweaving of the divine will, human resistance to it, and the divine response of judgement and mercy that characterizes human history as a whole, in its as yet unfinished journey towards its final destiny.

9
The longing for God

The Jews did not think of God only as the creator, the giver of the Law, and the Lord of history. Such a God might be remote, imperious and fearful. But the God of the prophets is a passionate God, with whom his covenant people are passionately involved. The Psalmist sings, 'As a deer longs for flowing streams, so my soul longs for you, O God' (Psalm 42.1). The prophets sang and danced before the Lord in ecstatic rapture, and the praise of God is no mere formal obeisance. True knowledge of God is like a passionate embrace, like the first flush of falling in love: 'I adjure you, O daughters of Jerusalem, if you find my beloved, tell him this: I am faint with love' (Song of Solomon 5.8).

The prophets could speak of the marriage of God and the soul, and that is perhaps the basic experience on which prophetic religion is founded, an experience to which they look forward in even more intense form: 'You show me the path of life. In your presence there is fullness of joy' (Psalm 16.11).

At the same time, the prophets were keenly aware of the estrangement of human lives from God, and the sense of pointlessness this engendered: 'Vanity of vanities, says the Teacher, all is vanity' (Ecclesiastes 12.8). The innocent are destroyed by the evils of the wicked, and the thoughts of the wise perish in dust. Often, instead of the joyful sense of God, there is only the desolation of emptiness and absence: 'My God, my God, why have you forsaken me?' (Psalm 22.1). Then the emptiness of the heart could be filled with bitterness, and even faith could be turned to hatred: 'Do I not hate those who hate you, O LORD? And do I not loathe those who rise up against you?' (Psalm 139.21), writes the Psalmist, overcome with anger at the cruelty of those who torture and massacre their enemies.

So the wisdom writings of the Hebrew Bible range over the whole spectrum of human emotions, from love to hate, from despair to hope, from a sense of intimacy with God to a sense of impenetrable mystery. Sometimes the biblical writers come near to despair at the futility of a life where God seems absent (in parts of Ecclesiastes, for instance), and sometimes (as in Job) they almost give up the attempt to understand the goodness of God in a world filled with innocent suffering. But they have heard of, and sometimes themselves felt, an experience of God that brings 'the fullness of joy', and that has left in them an intense longing for God.

So in the Psalms, written over a long period and through many misfortunes as well as times of happiness, the underlying mood is of praise and thanks to the God who is not only wise, powerful and beautiful, but is also 'him whom my soul loves' (Song of Solomon 3.1), and the one who says to Israel, 'I will take you for my wife in righteousness and in justice, in steadfast love and in mercy' (Hosea 2.19).

The God of Abraham, Isaac and Jacob is a God who loves each individual passionately, and who pleads with each of us to love in return. That is the personal heart of faith in God – not mere intellectual belief, but a surrender of the heart to the Beloved, whose 'love is strong as death' (Song of Solomon 8.6), who calls us to give our lives to love, and whose promise that we shall feel the divine love in its fullness enables each of us to say, 'I shall behold your face in righteousness; when I awake I shall be satisfied, beholding your likeness' (Psalm 17.15).

10
The dream of a Messiah

Many prophets were members of bands of ecstatic singers or court officials whose job was to foretell good or bad fortune. As is regrettably true in all human affairs, some were opportunists, frauds or political sycophants.

But the Hebrew Bible picks out 15 prophets who stood out from the rest, between the eighth and sixth centuries BC, by their fearless loyalty to God and their determination to tell unpopular truths. Their oracles, poems, historical records and exhortations were collected with other works by writers now unknown, and edited into the books of the 'Latter Prophets'.

These prophets lived at the times when first Israel and then Judah were about to be overwhelmed by the imperial powers of Assyria and Babylon, during the exile in Babylon, and immediately after the return to Jerusalem. They denounced the corruption of Israel and Judah, and warned of imminent military disaster. They encouraged people to return to their ancient faith, the passionate love of God and selfless care for the poor. In the darkest days they taught that the great empires of the North would in their turn be overthrown, and pictured a future in which God would eliminate evil and establish Israel again in her own land, as a centre of reconciliation from which the love of God could spread throughout the world.

In poetry of frightening power the great prophets proclaim the ruthless judgement of God on all evil, both in Israel and in her enemies, bringing terror and utter destruction. But they also foretell a time of renewal, when all the world will turn to God and live, and when Israel will discover her true vocation: 'The days are surely coming, says the LORD, when I will make a new covenant with the house of Israel . . . I will put my law within them, and I will write it on their hearts; and I will be their God, and they shall be my people' (Jeremiah 31.31–33).

The people of Israel will be the priests of the earth: 'My house shall be called a house of prayer for all peoples' (Isaiah 56.7), and 'nations that do not know you shall run to you' (Isaiah 55.5). All the scattered tribes of Israel will return to Jerusalem, from all the corners of the earth: 'The ransomed of the LORD shall return, and come to Zion with singing; everlasting joy shall be upon their heads' (Isaiah 51.11).

As the prophets looked ahead to the ultimate triumph of goodness, they sketched a vision of a time at which creation itself would be renewed: 'the lion shall eat straw like the ox. . . . They will not hurt or destroy on all my holy mountain; for the earth will be full of the knowledge of the LORD as the waters cover the sea' (Isaiah 11.7–9).

As they envisioned this time, which fulfils and yet is beyond historical time, they also imagined a mysterious figure who would bring near the knowledge and rule of God: 'My servant David shall be king over them . . . and my servant David shall be their prince for ever' (Ezekiel 37.24–25). The royal dynasty of Judah would be renewed and would last for ever. Yet the coming king would in a strange way be 'a man of suffering and acquainted with infirmity' (Isaiah 53.3). Through his sufferings he would bring his people close to God: 'The righteous one,

my servant, shall make many righteous, and he shall bear their iniquities'
(Isaiah 53.11).

With that vision of a suffering king who would renew the earth and
restore Israel to her true vocation of living in true union with God, Hebrew
prophecy came to an end. The institution of prophecy died out, as the
people of Israel endured successive waves of imperial conquest. But
the idea of a Messiah, God's 'anointed', empowered by God to deliver
Israel from her oppressors and renew God's covenant of the heart, did
not die.

The Messianic kingdom is still the dream of Israel, though how and
when it will come about is regarded as wrapped in mystery. It was into
that atmosphere of a nation living under military oppression, longing
for divine judgement on the brutal and cruel powers of the world, and
hoping for divine deliverance and renewal for Israel, that Jesus (the Greek
form of the Hebrew name Joshua) was born. The claim his disciples were
to make was that Jesus was the promised Messiah. For many Jews this
claim was and for most it still is unacceptable, for peace and justice have
clearly not yet been established in the world. But Jesus' life and teaching was to transform the idea of God's kingdom in a radical way, and
to take faith in the God of Abraham, Isaac and Jacob throughout the
known world.

Without the patriarchs and prophets of the people of Israel, Christian
faith would not exist. For Christians, Judaism has its own authenticity,
and God will not abandon the ancient covenant with the sons of
Israel – 'God has not rejected his people whom he foreknew' (Romans 11.2).
But there is also a new covenant, open to the whole world, founded
on belief that Jesus is indeed the Messiah (in Greek, the Christ), the one
who was foretold by the great prophets of the Hebrew faith.

Jesus in the Gospels

11
The kingdom

Almost all the information we have about Jesus is in the four Gospels,
apart from a few references in Acts and the New Testament letters. The
Gospels were compiled by people who believed Jesus was the Messiah,
using earlier oral traditions, in the light of their belief that Jesus had

been raised from death and so vindicated as God's anointed. Scholars generally think that Mark is the earliest Gospel, dating from around AD 65 to 76, and that it gives the most reliable portrait of the historical Jesus. Matthew and Luke provide rather more elaborated documents, which express their own distinctive viewpoints. The Gospel of John is later, perhaps from around 90 to 100 AD, and is more like a theological meditation on the person of Jesus. The editor puts into the mouth of Jesus what are more likely to be early Church reflections on the role and status of the Messiah, as risen Lord of the Church.

The Gospels thus give us four views of how the early Church saw Jesus. They certainly refer back to a historical person, the main outlines of whose life and teachings are probably faithfully remembered. But they are rather different portraits of Jesus, a Jesus seen through the eyes of very different believers, all of whom believed they had experienced the presence of the risen Lord, and read that experience back into the historical records.

For a modern biographer, they no doubt leave much to be desired. We have no record of what Jesus looked like, and we almost never have his actual words, which were probably in Aramaic, not the Greek of the Gospels. Yet what the Gospels give us is four different responses, all expressing total trust and devotion to a figure whose charismatic power, wisdom and love have transformed human understanding of God, and changed the course of world history.

It seems certain that Jesus' central message was that 'the time is fulfilled, and the kingdom of God has come near; repent, and believe in the good news' (Mark 1.15). This message explicitly refers to the fulfilment to which the Old Testament prophets had looked forward, and asserts that God's rule has come near to those who stand in the presence of Jesus (Matthew 12.28: 'If it is by the Spirit of God that I cast out demons, then the kingdom of God has come to you').

The 'fulfilment of time' is the prophets' longed-for liberation from evil and union with the love of God. The 'kingdom' is the rule (*basileia*) of God in the lives of men and women, and that rule is made actual in the life of Jesus, the one in whom God's rule is complete. Jesus calls those who hear him to repent – to turn their minds from love of self and indifference to others – and to believe – to accept that Jesus reveals what God's love is, and to receive from him the power to be liberated from self and discover in God the perfection of love.

This good news both is and is not what the prophets expected. It is, because the prophets' dream that human nature would be freed from hatred, greed and inordinate desire, and united to God in passionate love, finds in Jesus its perfect realization in history. It is not, because Jesus does not offer the military overthrow of the Roman occupation and the physical return of the twelve tribes to Jerusalem in triumph, to found a united nation of the sons of Israel.

So Jesus is a strange Messiah. While fulfilling the prophetic hopes of Israel, he also transforms them almost beyond recognition. The liberation he announces is not from political enemies, but from the powers of evil within the heart. The renewal of the covenant he brings is not the building of a physical temple in Jerusalem, but the founding of a community of the Spirit of God, by which God's rule is brought near to the whole world. The kingship he offers is not in the splendour of a royal palace, but in the service of the poor and the healing of the sick. And he enters into his reign, not by a triumphal entry into Jerusalem, but by way of a humiliating death outside the walls of the holy city.

If this is the place on earth where God's love is truly shown, it is a more costly, precarious and vulnerable thing than most of us could ever have imagined. This Messiah is the suffering king, his arms outstretched on the cross to embrace the whole world in costly and limitless love.

12
The infancy narratives

Many religious teachers are credited with supernatural or miraculous births. So it is not totally surprising that Matthew and Luke both provide accounts of Jesus being conceived without a human father, after a visitation by an angel. Luke tells the story from the point of view of Mary, mother of Jesus, and Matthew does so from the viewpoint of Joseph, betrothed to Mary. What is interesting in both accounts is what spiritual meaning they were trying to convey. Both contain genealogies tracing Jesus' ancestry from Abraham. The lists differ in many ways, and so are obviously not literally accurate, but their main point is to place Jesus in the royal line of descent from David, and to establish him as the fulfilment of the whole of biblical history up to that time.

In Luke, the angel Gabriel, who stands in the presence of God, appears to the devout priest Zechariah, and to Mary, announcing to the former the miraculous birth of John the Baptist, who will be 'filled with the Holy Spirit' (1.15), and to the latter the even more miraculous birth of Jesus, who is not just filled with, but generated by the Spirit, not by any human father. Angels appear, glorifying God and telling of the birth of the Messiah, to a group of shepherds, who represent ordinary people on the fringe of respectable society. After Jesus' birth, the righteous prophets Simeon and Anna, who were looking for 'the consolation of Israel' (2.25), declare that they have found the object of their hope in Jesus, the glory of Israel and light of the world.

Thus Luke portrays Jesus as announced by angels, recognized as Messiah by devout priests, prophets and the simple peasants of Israel, and as wholly unique in human history, conceived by the Spirit and born of a virgin mother. His account is a highly literary construction, containing three poems modelled closely on passages in the Hebrew Bible, and put into the mouths of Zechariah, Mary and Simeon, that have become important parts of Christian worship, as the Benedictus, Magnificat and Nunc Dimittis of the Daily Office.

Luke's attempt to locate Jesus' birth at a specific point in history, by relating it to a census taken when Quirinius was governor of Syria, faces the difficulty that there was almost certainly no such census, and that Quirinius only became governor some years after the death of King Herod in 4 BC. Unlike Matthew, Luke makes Nazareth the home town of Joseph and Mary, and the supposed census is a way of getting them to Bethlehem, where the Messiah was expected to be born. Most biblical scholars see this prologue to Luke's Gospel as a finely written literary narrative intended to depict Jesus' role as destined King of Israel, who will deliver Israel from all her enemies. Jesus is born, not by any human will, but solely by the Spirit of God and the consent of Mary. She is the symbol of 'the virgin Israel', from whom God can still bring new life and a new creation. Jesus is that new creation, Spirit-born and Spirit-led, the true shepherd-king, born in a cattle-stall yet known from the first as the Saviour of the world.

Matthew presents a different narrative, but with the same general intention. He does not share Luke's interest in John the Baptist, nor does he have Luke's poetic gifts. His interest is more in showing that Jesus fulfilled various Old Testament prophecies. An angel appears to Joseph, telling him of the miraculous conception of Jesus (Matthew quotes the Greek version of Isaiah's prophecy, that 'a virgin shall conceive' – Isaiah 7.14 says in the original Hebrew only that a 'young woman' shall conceive). Then some astrologers or wise men, following a star, bring gifts to Jesus in his house in Bethlehem – so Matthew depicts Jesus' fulfilment of the hopes of all the peoples of the world. In Matthew there is naturally no mention of an inn or of a stable, since Mary and Joseph already lived in Bethlehem. Finally, Joseph flees to Egypt with his family, to escape the anger of King Herod, and after Herod's death he returns, but makes his home in the north, in Nazareth, for fear of further persecution. So, Matthew says, the prophecy was fulfilled, 'Out of Egypt have I called my son' (Hosea 11.1 – originally a recollection of Israel's escape from slavery in Egypt).

Matthew is presenting in dramatic form, rather more prosaically than Luke, Jesus as the fulfilment both of the prophecies of Israel and of the religious hopes of the world. Jesus, like Moses, is miraculously saved from an early death. He comes from Egypt into the wilderness, where he is tempted but overcomes temptation. He conquers the forces of evil, disease and sickness in Canaan. He will suffer as Israel suffered throughout her history. But he is destined to save the people of the world from their sins. Jesus' life recapitulates the history of Israel, and thus he becomes in his own person the true Israel, from whom the salvation of the whole world will come.

In these two rather different infancy narratives, we can see the general character of the Gospels rather clearly. They are works composed to bring out the meaning of Jesus' person and ministry, in the light of experiences of his living presence in the early Church. They use material drawn from the Hebrew Bible, and they almost certainly draw on reminiscences of those who had known Jesus. But they are creative in their use of such materials, and we have to say that it is fairly certain that many of the incidents they record are purely imaginative.

The best way to read the accounts is not to ask if they really happened precisely like that, but to ask what the writers were trying to convey, and whether that has anything to say to us in our own spiritual lives. The question about literal fact is almost always the wrong one. The question about spiritual meaning takes us back to our own relationship with God, and the ways in which God can speak to us through these narratives. The Gospels are precious to Christians because they are nearer to the remembered person of Jesus than anything else we have. But the person of Jesus is precious because it mediates to us the presence and character and power of God. And that can be so, even if we must always confess that we can never know exactly what happened either at the birth of Jesus or at any other moment of his life. The Gospels can never tell us that. They tell us how the risen Christ can mediate God to us now, liberate us from self and restore us to union with God. That is all we can obtain; that has to be, and it is, enough.

13
Miracles

Jesus lived out most of his life in Galilee, a largely rural northern territory of an insignificant Roman province.

Jesus taught in the local synagogues, and Luke represents him as applying Messianic prophecies to himself from the first – 'The Spirit of the Lord is upon me, because he has anointed me . . . to proclaim the year of the Lord's favour' (Luke 4.18–19). Jesus saw himself as designated by God to inaugurate a new, creative and liberating spiritual reality. The Synoptic Gospels capture what was new about this by having John the

Baptist say of Jesus, 'he will baptize you with the Holy Spirit' (Luke 3.16). He was no ordinary prophet.

His teaching aroused controversy, especially in his local community. Nevertheless, he gathered around him a fairly large group of disciples, and an inner core of twelve. He taught them, and eventually sent them out to proclaim the 'drawing near' of God's kingdom, to call the people to turn to God, and to heal those who were physically or mentally ill (many such healings were interpreted as 'exorcisms of demons' in that society).

Miracles, extraordinary physical signs of divine presence and power, were an important part of Jesus' ministry. Thirty-five miracles of Jesus are recorded in the Gospels. Twenty-three of them are miracles of healing, showing the will and power of God to make human lives whole in mind and body.

In the Hebrew Bible, the prophets, men who were close to God in knowledge and holiness of life, were often mediators of divine wisdom and power. Though as humans their powers were limited, by their closeness to God they were places where divine power could be manifested. So Jesus, who was uniquely close to God, being filled with the Spirit of God, was in his own person a place where God's power to make whole was manifested in a spectacular way. Jesus' healing miracles are natural expressions of his compassion, of his unique unity with God, and of the 'immanence of the kingdom', the presence of God's rule in his person. What they show is that God's will is always to forgive and heal, not to judge and destroy.

Three times Jesus is said to have brought the dead back to life. Again the point is to show God's life-giving power, which cannot be defeated by death.

Nine miracles involve Jesus' power over nature. He calmed the storm and walked on water, produced food for people to eat, knew where fish were to be found, and turned water into wine. These miracles have symbolic significance (miracles are called 'signs' in John's Gospel). They reflect God's power over the waters of chaos (Psalm 65.7 says of God, 'You silence the roaring of the seas'), or God's provision of manna for the people of Israel in the wilderness. The catch of fish symbolizes the entrance of people into the kingdom, and the transformation of water into wine symbolizes the pouring of new, intoxicating life into what had become in the hands of many the over-familiar purity laws of the Hebrew Bible.

In addition to the miracles performed by Jesus, the Gospels record three major miracles centred on his person – his birth from a virgin, his transfiguration, and his resurrection from the dead. Matthew and Luke recount the story of the virgin birth as a way of stating that in Jesus a new creation, a new union of divine and human, was effected. Of this three things should be said: we will never be able to tell whether this account is literally true; the infancy narratives are primarily imaginative writings, so the character of the text points away from literal truth; and a virgin birth is not at all necessary for Jesus' unique unity with God. This is a case where we might say that the literal truth of the miracle is inessential to the importance of the spiritual truth conveyed, though it cannot be dogmatically denied.

The Synoptic Gospels all recount the transfiguration of Jesus, when Peter, James and John saw him wreathed in dazzling light, talking with Moses and Elijah, and heard a voice from a cloud confirming his divine sonship. In the Gospel narratives, this is a dramatically important event, confirming Jesus' vocation to fulfil the Law and the prophets. It is recorded as a visionary experience, and foreshadows to some extent the resurrection appearances.

Those appearances are in a different category, however, for their actual occurrence does seem to be important for Christian belief. Even then, their precise nature must remain unknown, and it is enough to say that the disciples must have experienced the presence of the risen Lord in an intense and convincing manner. The written accounts we possess share the dramatic and literary character of the Gospels in general, and are better taken as imaginative presentations of the fact of the resurrection than as literal descriptions of it.

We cannot know to what extent the Gospel miracles literally occurred, though Jesus must have been known as a great healer and exorcist. We might expect that a teacher who was so close to God would show extraordinary signs of divine power. And it is important to note that the recorded miracles all show God's will for human healing, well-being and life. When two apostles wished to call down fire on villages that had rejected Jesus, some manuscripts of Luke record that Jesus said, 'You do not know what spirit you are of, for the Son of Man has not come to destroy the lives of human beings, but to save them' (Luke 9.56). The miracles are thus signs of salvation and new life. Nevertheless, humans are prone to exaggeration and to the literalizing of metaphorical statements (the cursing of the fig tree in Matthew 21.18–22 looks like a literalization, perhaps of a remark of Jesus about Jeremiah 8.13 – 'When I wanted to gather them, says the LORD, there are no grapes on the vine, nor figs on the fig tree'. In Luke's Gospel, the fig-tree incident occurs as a parable – Luke 13.6–9).

So perhaps we should just say that Jesus was a man of charismatic healing power and wisdom, but we cannot tell how far the miracles attributed to him were literal events. What matters is that the life of God was mediated in and through him, and his life manifested in extraordinary ways the presence and power of God. That power is unequivocally given for healing and new life. The God who is known in Jesus is not a God of anger and destruction, but a God who wills to make human lives whole.

14
Parables

Remarkably little of Jesus' teaching has been preserved. He never wrote a book, and the sayings in the Gospels are probably only a small selection from his teachings. According to the Synoptic Gospels (Matthew, Mark and Luke, called 'synoptic' because they agree fairly closely on Jesus' life and teaching, and can usefully be read alongside each other) Jesus taught, at least in public, in parables. These range from striking metaphors to allegories and stories with a moral or spiritual message. Their meaning is often obscure, and according to Mark, Jesus used parables so that outsiders 'may indeed listen, but not understand' (Mark 4.12). Only the disciples were given 'the mystery of the kingdom of God' concealed in the parables (Mark 4.11).

In Mark's Gospel, the two main parables are of the sower (Mark 4.3–9) and the wicked tenants of the vineyard (Mark 12.1–9). The first is about different responses to the good news of the kingdom – rejection, lack of perseverance, deflection by desire, and fidelity. The second concerns the tenants of a vineyard (Israel), who beat or kill those sent to collect the produce, including even the son of the owner. The tenants are eventually ejected, and the vineyard given to others. Shorter parables in Mark picture the kingdom as a rapidly growing tree or a field of wheat that grows until harvest time.

If 'the kingdom' is God's inward rule, Jesus is teaching that through him God intends to establish a new inward covenant of the heart, though few will be fully responsive to God's rule. Nevertheless, the community of the new covenant will rapidly grow and be fruitful, even if it is taken from the religious leaders of Israel and given to others.

Matthew adds a number of parables, which stress that 'the kingdom' is a community, in which good and bad live together. But there will be a judgement, when good and bad are separated, and the bad are excluded or suffer torment. Matthew insists on the necessity of works of practical charity, of forgiving others, and of using the gifts God gives. But he also insists that God seeks out sinners and gives much more than anyone deserves, and that the rewards of the kingdom, of life in the Spirit, outweigh anything else imaginable. Matthew's distinctive emphases are well illustrated in the parable of the sheep and the goats (Matthew 25.31–46), a terrifying picture of the Last Judgement, when all will be judged before the throne of God according to their works.

Luke records more parables, the tone of which is set by the three great stories of the good Samaritan (Luke 10.30–37), the prodigal son (Luke 15.11–32), and the rich man and Lazarus (Luke 16.19–31). God's love, these parables show, is universal, limitless, costly, forgiving, and compassionate. God's rule in the heart, if it is complete, produces in us such love. And if God's own love is like that, we see that the 'torment' the indifferent suffer is not some external punishment, but their realization that they have excluded themselves from love, are lost in the darkness of their own self-regard, and are seared by the flames of their own insatiable desires. We also have good reason to hope that God will never abandon them, but will continue to go to any lengths to turn their hearts back to God. In Luke's parable, the rich man in torment begins to think of others, and pray that they may be spared. As he does so, we may think that the chasm that separates him from Lazarus already begins to shrink. For God is both just and merciful; and the consensus of the parables is that God's mercy infinitely outweighs any strict requirements of justice.

The recorded parables of Jesus show the rigour of the demands of divine love, but also the limitlessness of the divine compassion. They speak of a new Davidic kingdom, in which the Spirit is poured out to rule the hearts of men and women, which promises a joy beyond compare, which is always compromised in history by human indifference, fear and selfish desire, but which will endure for ever. This is a kingdom in which Jesus himself will reign. But how and in what way this can be is the mystery of the kingdom, which only the disciples can discern, gradually and imperfectly, as they seek to follow their Lord with fervent faith.

15
Beatitudes

Matthew writes more of judgement than any other Gospel writer, and in his Gospel there is five times as much outer darkness, weeping and gnashing of teeth as in Luke. Yet it is in Matthew's Gospel that the 'Sermon on the Mount', the most penetrating record of Jesus' moral teaching, is to be found. Matthew has collected together many sayings of Jesus and formed them into a sermon on the divine Law. Like Moses, but, Matthew implies, with even greater authority, Jesus preaches from a 'mountain'. He does not give a new Law. Indeed, he stresses that the old Law remains in force (Matthew 5.18: 'Until heaven and earth pass away, not one letter, not one stroke of a letter, will pass from the law'). But he interprets the Law in a radical and authoritative way.

The sermon begins with nine Beatitudes, Jesus' description of true happiness. True happiness is not luxuriating in wealth. It lies with the poor, those who mourn, the humble, the hungry, the merciful, the pure in heart, the peacemakers, and those who are unjustly persecuted or reviled. How can that be? They are truly happy because they will possess the kingdom, they will be comforted, and they will see God.

Jesus' moral teaching begins with a promise, but that promise is not that if you lack a swimming pool now, you will get a big one in heaven. It is that if you obey the divine Law, you will experience union with God, a happiness outweighing all others. This does not make the Law just a means to happiness. On the contrary, the Law defines what true happiness is – loving God with all your heart, and being loved by God. Jesus' promise is that, even if you do not seem to experience that love now, even if you suffer poverty and injustice because of your obedience to the law of love, you will come to know and love God fully, to live in the presence of God.

The divine Law is not a set of arbitrary commands. The divine Law defines happiness as living in love, and defines love as supremely fulfilling personal relationship. Jesus promises that such relationship will be the reward of those who 'strive first for the kingdom of God' (Matthew 6.33). Jesus' own presence is the promise of a love that completes human happiness. But in this world the way to that happiness may well lie, as it was to do for Jesus himself, through suffering and death. Luke includes some of this teaching in his Gospel, mostly in chapter 6. In his version of the Beatitudes, the poor, the hungry, and those who mourn are starkly contrasted with the rich, well-fed and satisfied, for their positions will be completely reversed. The hierarchies of this world will be turned upside down when the kingdom comes: 'the last will be first, and the first will be last' (Matthew 20.16).

This is not 'pie in the sky when you die', a way to get the oppressed to accept their lot for the sake of a pretended happiness hereafter. This is Jesus' definitive promise of life with God for those who now perhaps glimpse God faintly and from afar, but who seek to love God out of sheer awareness of God's supreme goodness, who seek to live for the sake of good alone.

It would be a mistake to take this teaching too literally, as though the rich will be punished simply for being rich. But it would also be a mistake not to take it seriously, for God's priorities are not those of 'the world', the complex of greed and ambition that is such a marked feature of human society. There can be little doubt that Jesus' teaching is good news for the poor and the socially despised, and is severely critical of the arrogant and the uncaring rich.

His teaching is phrased in dramatic exaggerations that command attention by their very extremity. But the basic meaning is that the rich should use their wealth wisely, and not pursue it for its own sake. The oppressed should not despair, for they are promised companionship with God, a 'pearl of great value' (Matthew 13.46), worth more than everything else anyone could have.

The message of the Beatitudes is that the highest of all goals is God. Every goal that does not include that is in the end empty. Those who sincerely pursue that goal will achieve what they desire. The promise of such eternal love is the good news of the kingdom that draws near in the person of Jesus.

16
The Law of God

According to Matthew, Jesus taught his hearers that the Law should be obeyed, but he gave the Law a radical interpretation. This is set out in the five great Antitheses in the Sermon on the Mount, sayings which all begin: 'You have heard . . .', and conclude: 'But I say to you . . .'.

Jesus replaces a literal interpretation of strict legal rules with much more demanding ideals for attitudes of the heart. It is not just murder that is forbidden. It is all anger, insult and lack of respect for others. Adultery, sex with another man's wife, is taken to refer to all lustful thoughts, all thoughts that treat others as no more than objects for sexual pleasure. It is also extended to divorce for trivial or selfish reasons. The prohibition on oath-breaking now enjoins complete honesty, a prohibition on deceit in thought and intention. The restriction of vengeance to proportionate injury is overridden by a total prohibition of revenge, and the cultivation of an attitude of universal benevolence. Love of neighbours is extended to love of enemies and prayer for oppressors.

What Jesus demands of his disciples is that they should be without anger, without destructive sexual desire, without deceit, without any trace of vengeance or resentment, and without hatred. He goes on to say that they should not be proud or anxious or concerned about wealth or position, and should not make ostentatious display of their piety or righteousness. They should never sit in judgement on others. They should not pursue money, for 'you cannot serve God and Mammon [riches]' (Matthew 6.24). They should be, not masters, but the servants of all. Positively, they should always seek reconciliation and be prepared to forgive others, should honour other persons without discrimination, should seek the welfare of all without exception, and should, in short, 'do to others as you would have them do to you, for this is the Law and the prophets' (Matthew 7.12).

By this standard of morality, almost the whole human race stands condemned. It is possible for most of us to refrain from murder, adultery, oath-breaking and personally exacting excessive vengeance. Taken literally, it is possible to keep God's Law. Yet that Law can become restrictive and even inhumane. It can be used to license intolerance and violence – laws about the conquest of Canaan and the elimination of Canaanite religion can seem to legitimate religious warfare. It can lead to very exclusive and chauvinistic attitudes – the banning of foreign wives and laws of discrimination between Israelites and others can seem to license a sense of Jewish superiority. It can be inhumane and judgemental – the 'observant' can easily stand in judgement on others, and such things as keeping Sabbath regulations or the rigorous imposition of ancient penal codes can override common considerations of human welfare.

It is important to note that these would be negative and literalistic interpretations of the Law. Jewish use of the Law is more a matter of the development of underlying principles and creative judicial appeal to precedents than it is of unthinking application of ancient rules to modern cases. Jesus was not alone in criticizing interpretations of the Law that did not allow for a development of moral perception and for a determination to discern underlying principles rather than simply apply ancient rules.

Nevertheless, his interpretation of the Law was particularly clear and forceful in opposing all religious intolerance and violence ('love your enemies', Matthew 5.44), in opposing any chauvinistic sense of superiority ('the greatest among you will be your servant', Matthew 23.11), and in condemning the scrupulous but inhumane practice of religion ('Woe to you, scribes and Pharisees, hypocrites! For you tithe mint, dill, and cummin, and have neglected the weightier matters of the law: justice and mercy and faith' (Matthew 23.23).

The Gospels record that Jesus came into conflict with established religious teachers (called 'the scribes and Pharisees' in Matthew), not because he broke the Law, but because he interpreted it in a fully humane way. He healed, and defended the plucking of wheat, on the Sabbath, and taught that moral defilement is more important than ritual defilement. He criticized the self-righteousness and pride of those who thought they kept the Law. And he showed that obeying the Law truly, in the heart, is almost impossibly difficult.

It is possible to read Matthew's Gospel and think that it is uncomfortably moralistic, or that it propounds a new and extremely rigorous Law. But the deepest message of the Sermon on the Mount has been exactly captured by Paul, in the second letter to the Christians at

Corinth: 'The letter kills, but the Spirit gives life' (2 Corinthians 3.6). The law of the kingdom is the law of the heart, and only insofar as the Spirit lives in human hearts can we come near to seeing and doing what the Law of God requires.

17
Judgement

In the Hebrew Bible there was no clear belief in an after-life. So God's judgement and salvation had to take place in history. Judgement was seen by the prophets primarily as judgement on military oppressors, but it was broadened to include those who broke God's Law, and so separated themselves from union with God. Salvation similarly was freedom from oppression, but it was also life in the full knowledge and love of God.

Jesus, like the Pharisees, believed in the resurrection of the dead. So judgement and salvation came to be taken to occur after earthly death.

No mature spiritual view would think of judgement as torture imposed simply for past disobedience. But nor would it be fair for those who have killed and hated to live happily for ever. If the universe is morally ordered, there must be something like a law of moral compensation or desert – you will be treated as you treat others.

This is present in Jesus' teaching: 'For the Son of Man is to come with his angels in the glory of his Father, and then he will repay everyone for what has been done' (Matthew 16.27); 'For with the judgement you make you will be judged, and the measure you give will be the measure you get' (Matthew 7.2).

Yet in the Sermon on the Mount Jesus teaches that we should not resist evil, but turn the other cheek (Matthew 5.38), and that we should love our enemies and those who hate us (Matthew 5.44), and that in this way we will be 'perfect as your heavenly Father is perfect' (Matthew 5.48). At the very least, this means that God is not vengeful or vindictive, and will never cease to love us, even though we hate God.

That explicitly rules out strict retributive punishment ('an eye for an eye'), or any punishment that is a final cutting-off of divine love and does not express concern for our ultimate well-being. All divine 'punishment' must attend to what could correct our faults or teach us true compassion, not just mechanically do to us what we have done to others. And it must aim at bringing us back to God – it can never be solely retributive, harming us just because and to the degree that we have harmed others.

How can we hold these things together? We can do so only if we do not take retributive talk literally, as laying down unbreakable rules –

that is the whole point of Jesus' teachings about the divine Law in the Sermon on the Mount. It is rather that those who are indifferent to others must find out what it is like to be treated with indifference. They must learn empathy, real identification with the pain of others, that indifferent acts have caused. But empathy is not best learned by torturing someone. It is best learned by experiencing what it is like to be another person, so that you commit yourself to doing something, by effort and hard work, to make things better.

There are three conditions of merciful punishment. It must aim at changing character. It must require hard work to make restitution. And it must have the prospect of ending.

It is possible that character will not be changed, but will harden. Souls may sink further into hatred and greed. It will then be important that their hatred and greed bring them no advantage or satisfaction. They will become bitter, enraged individuals, forever seeking new pleasures and failing to be satisfied. They may be described as tormented and destroyed by the flames of their inordinate desires, or as locked into the darkness of their own loneliness and hatred of others. Even then, the possibility of escape remains, of discovering the unsatisfactoriness of their lives and vowing to change.

Could such a state continue for ever? Perhaps it would best be described as 'age-long' (the exact translation of *aionios*, the New Testament word usually translated as 'eternal'). It may continue as long as the person fails to feel the suffering of such an existence enough to want to change it.

Judgement, we might say, is a state in which it becomes clear what sorts of persons we really are – proud, resentful, self-deceiving and egoistic, or genuinely devoted to the welfare of others. The Gospels use two main metaphors to describe this state. The just, the penitent, the humble, the innocent, enter the kingdom, where they sit at a great feast with Abraham and the prophets. The selfish, the unforgiving, the arrogant, the cruel, are locked out in darkness. Or the just are gathered into a barn, while the unjust are thrown onto Gehenna, the flaming rubbish-dump outside Jerusalem.

Nobody thinks there will be a literal feast, or that we will live in a literal barn. We will not go into literal darkness or be thrown on a fire of burning rubbish. There will, however, be a division: on the one hand happiness and security, on the other loneliness, torment and destruction. Happiness is the state of those who are open to the love of God, and allow it to transform their lives into channels of love. Misery and torment is the state of those who put themselves first, and whose selves are tormented and destroyed by the passions they unleash.

Jesus teaches that these things are to some extent realized during this life. But they become clear and unambiguous in the life beyond this world. That is the judgement – not that God punishes us for ever without possibility of reprieve, but that we have to live with what we have made ourselves, which we have often managed to disguise from ourselves and others in this world.

Yet there is no limit to divine forgiveness – according to Matthew, 'Peter came up and said to him, "Lord, if another member of the church sins against me, how often should I forgive? As many as seven times?" Jesus said to him, "Not seven times, but, I tell you, seventy times seven' (Matthew 18. 21–22). Would God do less? So the door of repentance is never closed.

Regrettably, Christians have often misunderstood Jesus' teaching on judgement by taking his parables literally, and by letting the harshest-sounding texts (like Matthew 25.46: 'These will go away into eternal punishment, but the righteous into eternal life') become the key to interpreting the others.

But such texts cannot consistently be taken literally – we are not, after all, literally either ears of wheat or weeds. Matthew's 'punishment' may be eternal, or age-long, just as the fires of Gehenna never die, but it does not follow that we can never escape from that punishment or that unquenchable fire. And what is the reason for thinking that all can be freed from it? Most importantly, it is Jesus' teaching on what love requires – unlimited forgiveness, undying concern for the welfare of even those who hate you, and the costly love shown by the parable of the Good Samaritan. Those texts should be the key for interpreting all Jesus' parables concerning judgement. They unequivocally entail that 'it is not the will of my Father who is in heaven that one of these little ones should perish' (Matthew 18.14). If only they will repent, they will not be eternally lost.

Jesus stands in the tradition of the prophets of Israel, and he undoubtedly teaches that there will be a judgement, that the deeds of all will be exposed, and judged by the rigorous standards of divine self-giving love. By those standards, almost all will stand condemned. Such condemnation should not be taken lightly, for it means that we are unfit for the companionship of God, and locked into the flames of our own desires and the darkness of our misanthropy.

Yet precisely because it is divine love that judges us, and because divine love is limitlessly forgiving, we can be sure that repentance and renewal of mind is possible, even beyond death. Nevertheless we must not take it for granted, and perhaps the longer we leave it, the harder repentance becomes.

The idea of a limited time of punishment is suggested by three Gospel passages. In the Sermon on the Mount, Jesus tells a parable of being put in prison if you do not make friends with your accuser, and says, 'You will never get out till you have paid the last penny' (Matthew 5.26). In another parable, the prison metaphor is used again, and the unmerciful servant is put in prison 'till he should pay all his debt' (Matthew 18.34).

Luke records a parable of a servant who has not prepared for his master's return, and says, 'That servant who knew his master's will, but did not make ready or act according to his will, shall receive a severe beating. But he who did not know and did what deserved a beating, shall receive a light beating' (Luke 12.47–48).

These are only parables, but they suggest that there are different degrees of punishment, just as there are different degrees of reward. And the punishments are of limited duration. When the doctrine of purgatory developed in the Church, it built on such texts as these, speaking of punishment as a sort of probation which is meant to lead eventually to union with God. Jesus' insistent and repeated teaching on the unqualified and unlimited nature of love strongly suggests that Sheol or Hades (the world of the dead), Gehenna or the Outer Darkness are more like purgatorial fire than like everlasting hell. As Mark's Gospel says, 'Everyone will be salted with fire' (Mark 9.49). It is possible that some human souls will irrevocably reject the love of God. But it is also possible that the power of self will be broken, and that the souls in darkness will come to accept the forgiving love of God. That is what God desires, and the good news Jesus proclaimed is that the love of God draws near to inspire our acceptance.

18

Apocalypse

'Apocalypse' originally meant 'revelation', but it has come to stand for a particular style of writing that was popular in the time between the Old and New Testaments, and in the lifetime of Jesus and beyond. That style strikes some of us as very obscure and over-dramatic today, though something like it can be found in many science-fiction and horror stories. It uses fantastic cosmic imagery to depict historical and political events. It uses often lurid symbols to speak of an imminent cataclysmic judgement on human evil, and the dramatic arrival of God or God's deputy on to the world stage, to engage in a decisive conflict with the devil and bring about the triumph of the forces of good. The Synoptic Gospels (but not John) use apocalyptic images.

The crucial question is, in what sense did Jesus use such images? Of course, we cannot know that. But it seems right to use the general tenor of his other recorded teachings to help to interpret the apocalyptic ones. As with all Jesus' recorded teachings, we cannot be certain what is really original with him, and what has been embroidered, modified or even invented by the transmitters of the tradition or by the Gospel editors. But it is possible to see how Jesus could have used apocalyptic images, largely in a metaphorical sense, to portray his mission to Israel and its consequences.

Mark 13 presents one version of the Synoptic Apocalypse. Jesus speaks of a coming time of troubles, of wars, earthquakes and famines. He speaks of the persecution of his followers, and of the destruction of Jerusalem and its Temple. He warns his disciples not to be misled by false Messiahs, saying that 'the coming of the Son of Man' will be sudden and unmistakeable, but that the gospel must be preached 'to all nations' first. He speaks of the darkening of the sun and moon, the fall of the stars from the sky, and the coming of 'the Son of Man' in clouds with glory, who will send out his angels to gather in 'the elect' from all the earth. This will happen, he says, within a generation, so it will be soon, but at a day and hour that is totally unexpected, so the disciples need to 'keep awake' and be watchful at all times.

These sayings can only be interpreted sensibly by studying the Old Testament passages upon which they depend, and by noting how those passages are to be interpreted. In the Synoptic Gospels, the phrase 'Son of Man' is used by Jesus to refer to himself. Many scholars take the reference to be to Daniel 7. 13–14, where the prophet has a vision of 'one like a son of man' who comes on the clouds and is given rule over all peoples for ever. In Daniel, the 'son of man' stands for the 'holy ones of Israel', who will, after great struggle, overcome the militaristic powers of the earth and reign for ever. If Jesus applied this term to himself, he could have been seeing himself as the personal representative or symbol of Israel, the one who, after bitter struggle, would overcome all evil on earth.

The 'coming of the Son of Man' will then be the final conquest of evil. This will come only after 'the stars have fallen from the sky' – a reference to an oracle of Isaiah (13.1–22). This speaks of God's judgement on evil, but it specifically predicts the downfall of Babylon, the destroyer of Israel. The prophet then says that, after this downfall, which is pictured as the desolation of the whole earth and of the powers of the heavens themselves, God will restore Israel, so that 'the house of Israel will possess the nations' (Isaiah 14.2).

This oracle of Isaiah is written in hugely exaggerated terms, depicting a political defeat as a cosmic battle, and depicting the return of a few exiles to Jerusalem as Israel's rule over the whole earth. Such apocalyptic writing might be termed 'cosmic hyperbole'. There is judgement and there is hope, but the judgement is not as total and cosmic as a literal reading of the oracle would suggest, and the hope is not as crudely nationalistic and triumphalist as a literal reading would make it seem.

There is, however, a double focus in Isaiah's oracle. The historical reality of the fall of Babylon and the return of the Jewish exiles is seen as a foreshadowing of events at the end of historical time, when evil will be totally defeated, and the 'true Israel', those who love God fully, will participate in the glorious love of God. But to discern that 'ultimate' meaning all traces of nationalism and vengefulness need to be removed. It is not just Israel's enemies, but also all hypocrisy and pride within Israel, that will be eliminated. It is not that Israel will make all her former enemies slaves, but that God alone will rule, and Israel will be slaves of God.

If we now apply these lessons to the Synoptic Apocalypse, we can see first a historical reference. Jesus predicts that Jerusalem and the Temple will be destroyed, and Israel as a national state will cease to exist – that is the element of judgement. But, like Isaiah, he predicts that there will be a renewal of hope. As in Daniel, the 'coming of the Son of Man' is the birth of a new community of the 'holy ones of Israel', but now drawn by 'angels', the messengers of the gospel, from the four corners of the earth. This, for those who have eyes to see, is the birth of the Church of Christ, the new community that is the body of Christ, and in which Christ lives and rules for ever.

All those things happened within the lifetime of the generation to whom Jesus spoke. But there is also, as in Isaiah, the double focus. At the end of historical time, all evil will be extinguished, and Jesus will be seen as he truly is, in the glory of the Father. As with Isaiah, all exclusivism and vengefulness need to be eradicated from this picture. It is not only the Church that inherits the kingdom, but all who turn to God for forgiveness. It is not the Church that will rule the world, for the Church is the company of those who serve. The Church is, or ought to be, the present foreshadowing in time of this supra-historical state.

For those in the Church of Christ, there remains a future hope, that the love of God seen in the person of Jesus will be clearly present and universally acknowledged. In fact we have no idea when this will be, and Jesus' recorded teachings vacillate between suggesting that it might be soon and counselling patience. The parables of the 'thief in the night' and the 'unexpectedly returning master of the house' (Matthew 24.42–51; Luke 12.35–46) often taken by literalizing readers of the Gospels to be statements that Jesus might return soon, are precisely parables, not literal predictions. Their point lies in the admonition that we must be awake and watchful at all times, not in their suggestion that Jesus might be a thief, or that he might literally return at any moment.

In fact, the earth might cease to exist at any moment, or it may continue for millions of years. Since we do not know, these parables teach that we should live as though the end might be soon, in the confidence that, be it soon or remote, life will not simply be extinguished. We shall see Christ as he is, and God's purpose for the world will ultimately be realized.

Confusion can be caused by running together the historical and the ultimate meanings of the Synoptic Apocalypse, or by trying to interpret these cryptic symbols literally. Things are much clearer if we distinguish the things that did happen in Jesus' own generation, and are described in the common symbolism of the prophetic oracles, from the things that belong to ultimate human destiny, and that cannot be depicted in any adequate way, even by symbols.

If we do that, we will not see Jesus as a mistaken prophet of the imminent end of history. We will see him as a prophet of a terrible and imminent historical catastrophe for Israel, but as introducing a new society, bound to a new covenant with God through him, that will grow throughout the whole earth, and that will bring the Spirit of God so near that it will rule within the human heart. That is the Messianic role of Jesus, for, as Luke puts it, 'The kingdom of God is not coming with things that can be observed; nor will they say, "Look, here it is!" or "There it is!" For, in fact, the kingdom of God is among [or: within] you' (Luke 17.20–21).

19
The death of Jesus

The Synoptic Gospels depict Jesus' ministry as evoking amazement and devotion among the ordinary people, but as arousing growing opposition among those described as the Pharisees, scribes and lawyers (or, in John's Gospel, simply as 'the Jews'). Jesus' harshest words are reserved for the religious establishment. He berates them for their pride and hypocrisy, their attachment to the fastidious application of regulations, their concern for such things as ritual washing and purification above ordinary human kindness and compassion, and their love of money and position.

They, for their part, were offended by the fact that he ate with tax-collectors and known sinners (Mark 2.16), that he failed to observe common fasting and purity rules (Mark 2.18), and that he healed and apparently condoned work (gathering grain to eat) on the Sabbath (Mark 3.2; 2.24). In doing such things he was not breaking the Law, but he was affronting a narrow and literalistic interpretation of the Law.

Jesus challenged the religious authorities, ejecting tradesmen from the Temple precinct, claiming the right to forgive sins (Mark 2.5; Luke 7.48), and, according to Matthew and Luke, claiming to have unique knowledge of God – 'No one [fully] knows the Father except the Son'

(Matthew 11.27; cf. Luke 10.22). He apparently spoke of the destruction of the Temple and the destruction of Jerusalem, even of a catastrophic end to the religious hierarchy of Judaea. It is not surprising that they plotted to silence his subversive teachings. The fact that his disciples regarded him as the divinely designated King of Israel – which the accounts of his entry into Jerusalem on a donkey suggest – provided them with the charge of political subversion that they needed to obtain a judicial Roman execution.

The crucifixion of Jesus has become a central symbol of the Christian faith. It was a cruel death, though not uniquely so, in the terrible history of our world. It was an innocent death, for Jesus had taught a message of God's forgiveness and limitless love, he had healed the sick, and he had worked among the poor and marginalized. But he was a threat to religious and social values, and he was killed in order to preserve order and tradition. Both religious and political leaders found it expedient to remove this threat.

But the crucifixion, for the disciples, was more than the cruel execution of a blameless radical. It was the torture and death of the Messiah by his own people and religion. Over his head on the cross were written the words 'King of the Jews'. And so, they believed, he was. With hindsight they applied to him the prophecy of Isaiah 53, which speaks of the suffering of God's chosen servant.

This figure, despised and rejected, has in fact 'borne our infirmities and carried our diseases' (Isaiah 53.4). By his sufferings, cruel and unjust, he 'shall make many righteous' (Isaiah 53.11). In fact, 'he was wounded for our transgressions', and 'through him the will of the LORD shall prosper' (Isaiah 53.5, 10). It is essential to Isaiah's vision that the servant should be righteous, and should be the one through whom God will bring about the divine purpose of salvation. Yet it is precisely through his suffering and self-offering that salvation will be realized.

In its original context in Isaiah, the 'servant' is almost certainly the people of Israel after the exile in Babylon, pictured as sick and despised. But the vocation of Israel, to be the means of reconciling the whole world to God, remains in place. In a bold and imaginative move, the prophet suggests that the suffering of Israel may itself be the means of the world's reconciliation. As the people patiently bear the worst that the world can do, their righteousness and faithfulness to God reveals that the real sickness is that of their persecutors. The world's sickness or iniquity is thus borne by Israel, whose prayers that God should forgive their persecutors are effective precisely because those prayers arise out of suffering and self-offering to God.

The disciples came to see the suffering and killing of the Messiah in these poetic terms. Jesus on the cross may seem to be infirm and disfigured, a common criminal. But in truth the real spiritual sickness and criminality is that of those who condemned him. Jesus remains innocent, righteous and faithful. He offers his life to God, as a prayer that his persecutors' rejection of God may be forgiven and set aside. He makes himself 'an offering for sin', a pure prayer of total self-offering, arising out of selfless love, that those who have caused such suffering might be freed from the sickness of sin and 'made whole'.

For disciples of Jesus, the cross is no longer a symbol of shame and cruelty. It becomes a symbol of the love of God, which shares in the sickness and estrangement and suffering that evil causes. It becomes a symbol of the sacrifice of total self-offering, of prayer tested to the uttermost yet unwaveringly offered so that 'the will of the Lord shall prosper'. And it becomes a symbol of the secret victory of divine love, which triumphs not through force but through compassion, self-sacrifice, and the constant and undefeated will to forgive.

If we are open to biblical scholarship, we may not know with certainty very much of what Jesus taught and did. All we know is what came to be said about him later by different groups of disciples. But one of the most certain facts of history, if only because it was so shocking and unexpected, is that Jesus, the Galilean prophet and proclaimer of God's kingdom, was put to death on a cross outside the walls of the Holy City. This death should have put an end to his prophetic claims. But in fact it came to be seen by his disciples as the culmination and fulfilment of his brief ministry. For in the cross of Jesus the disciples see a human life wholly prepared to accept rejection, torture and death in order to realize God's purpose of forgiveness and wholeness of life, to let God's kingdom break in to an estranged world. And in that cross they see more. They see the love of God itself, expressed and lived out in a short human life, so that it was God in person who took 'the punishment that made us whole' (Isaiah 53.5), and who 'was wounded for our transgressions, crushed for our iniquities'. If that is the depth and the extent of the love of God, then there is nothing in heaven or in earth, in life or in death, that will ever be able to prevail against it. And that is why, paradoxical as it seems, the death of Jesus is itself the good news of the victorious rule of God in the hearts of men and women.

20

The resurrection

It is almost unthinkable that the Christian faith would have come into existence if the disciples had not believed that they had experienced the presence of Jesus, raised from death and raised to glory. Experience of the risen Lord is at the heart of Christian faith. For millions of believers in every age, the risen Christ has communicated the presence and character of God in an inward, powerful and life-transforming way. But what was the character of the first resurrection appearances to the disciples?

The Gospel accounts are quite short, and they differ in detail. But overall they present the following story. The tomb where Jesus' body had been laid to rest was found to be empty, probably by some female disciples. Jesus appeared in visions, first to a group of women, but then to many disciples, in apparently physical form, over a period of a few weeks ('forty days' is a conventional expression for a period of time), after which the physical appearances ceased.

He appeared in a room in Jerusalem behind locked doors. He walked 'in another form' with two disciples for seven miles, without being recognized, until he broke bread and suddenly vanished. Matthew records that he appeared on a hill in Galilee, and John records an appearance by Lake Tiberias. The Synoptic Gospels record Jesus' commissioning of the disciples to preach the gospel to all nations, and Mark (in the longer ending that was appended to the Gospel) and Luke briefly recount that Jesus then ascended into heaven to sit at the right hand of God – a poetic account of his final departure from the earth and his completed spiritual unity with God the Father.

What is unique in these accounts is not that Jesus lived after death in another form – Jesus had taught that the Patriarchs were not dead, but lived with God (Luke 20.37–38). What is unique is that Jesus appeared in physical form to his disciples. Yet this was no ordinary physical form. It appeared and vanished at will, it appeared in different forms, it was not impeded by locked doors, but it could be touched and could, Luke says, consume food (Luke 24.43). According to Luke, Jesus had promised on the cross that the penitent thief would be with him that day 'in Paradise' (Luke 23.43). One of the New Testament letters states that 'He [Jesus] was put to death in the flesh, but made alive in the spirit, in which also he went and made a proclamation to the spirits in prison' (1 Peter 3.19).

After his physical death, it seems that Jesus entered Paradise and also the 'prison' in which the spirits of the dead were held – suggesting that the world of the dead, known as Sheol in the Hebrew Bible, has both gloomy and happy sectors, into both of which Jesus entered 'in the spirit'. It is interesting to note that he is said to have preached the gospel to the spirits in prison (1 Peter 4.6), which strongly suggests that the dead, as well as the living, can hear the gospel and repent. All these factors fit with Paul's description of the resurrection body as a 'body of spirit', as opposed to an earthly body. Paul stresses that the resurrection body will be quite unlike our present physical bodies, though there will be some causal connection between them – 'You do not sow the body that is to be, but a bare seed' (1 Corinthians 15.37).

Paul claimed a vision of the resurrected Jesus, and this is described by Luke in Acts not as an ordinary physical body, but as a blinding light (Acts 9.3). So it seems that Jesus' physical body was transformed into a body of spirit. The physical body disappeared from the tomb, but his spiritual body was able to appear in physical form to the disciples for short periods, until such appearances ceased, and the Spirit came upon the disciples with power at Pentecost, in a purely spiritual, non-physical form.

To those who think there is no reality other than this physical world, the resurrection must seem an impossibility. But for those who think there is a God, a supreme spiritual reality that is the cause of the whole physical universe, it will seem obvious that there is a spiritual realm as well as a physical realm. It will seem possible that human beings might live in such a spiritual realm after their physical deaths. And it will seem possible that such humans might appear in the physical world, if such is God's intention.

Jesus' resurrection appearances accomplished three things. First, they vindicated his designated role as a true prophet, and as something more: as one chosen by God to be the paradigm image and act of God in human history. Second, they confirmed his continuing existence as the Davidic King whose rule would never end, the one through whom God's rule in human hearts would continue to be mediated. Third, they disclosed God's final purpose for human lives and for the whole creation, that they and it would be renewed and transformed in a full spiritual union with God.

The resurrection of Jesus reveals the destiny of humanity, and reveals the way in which that destiny is to be realized. It is an event of unique importance in human history, and thus it is fitting that this manifestation of the spiritual world in the physical should have a form that is unique in recorded history.

It is unique, but it is not just a series of events that break all the known laws of nature. It is something that reveals in an extraordinary way the true spiritual basis of all physical nature, and the ultimate spiritual goal towards which all the laws of nature are directed. The resurrection of Jesus is not a bizarre divine interruption in a purely material universe. It is a disclosure of the ultimate nature of reality as spiritual, and of the final goal of the material universe as the perfected unity of all things in God.

21

Ascension and Pentecost

The Gospel of Luke records that after a number of appearances of the risen Lord, Jesus 'was carried up into heaven' as he blessed the disciples (Luke 24.51). The same writer gives a longer account in the book of Acts (1.9–11). Jesus was lifted up, and a cloud received him, and two men in white said that he would come 'in the same way as you saw him go' (that is, in spiritual form). Whether this is a symbolic or a literal account, the spiritual message is clear: the risen Christ no longer exists on earth and can no longer be expected to appear on earth. Christ, received into the Shekinah, the cloud of the presence of God, has taken humanity into the very heart of God. And at the consummation of human history, that same Christ will appear again.

Just as at the incarnation God 'descended' to share fully in the human condition by filling a human being with the divine Spirit, so at the ascension the human person of Jesus 'ascended' to the divine presence, thereby making humanity a participant in the divine nature. But this is not a dissolution of the human into the divine, and at the end of human history the transfigured humanity of Jesus will 'return', or again take an individualized form that will be recognized in a renewed human community.

What this form will be, either in Jesus or in ourselves, we do not know: 'what we will be has not yet been revealed. What we do know is this: when he is revealed, we will be like him, for we will see him as he is' (1 John 3.2). Humanity itself will be transformed by its completed unity with God; and Jesus, the paradigm of all whom God unites to the divine, will be known by all as the Saviour of the world, the King who serves and the Judge who heals by taking all his judicial sentences of condemnation upon himself (Isaiah 53.5).

Until that time the Spirit of God, who has always been present within creation to shape and order it to realize the divine purpose, and to inspire human minds and hearts to appreciate and understand it, is present to the Church in a new name and form. The creative Spirit of divine Wisdom becomes the redemptive Spirit of Christ, and as such the Spirit acts within human lives to shape them on the pattern of Christ, to unite them in fellowship, to free them from selfish desire, and to unite them inwardly in love to God.

At the feast of Pentecost, fifty days after the Passover when Jesus was crucified, many believers were gathered together in a house in Jerusalem, when with the sound of a violent wind, they were touched with flames of fire, and began to speak in strange languages (possibly a combination of 'speaking in tongues', in unintelligible speech, and of 'interpretation', by which hearers could translate such speech into their own native language. Peter and the apostles at once interpreted this as Jesus' promised gift of the Holy Spirit, which would fill them with divine power, endow them with divinely inspired forms of speech, and transform them with joy and an overwhelming sense of forgiveness and new life, which they were impelled to proclaim to others (Acts 2.1–36).

The book of Acts records that three thousand Jews who were in Jerusalem for the festival were baptized that day in the name of Jesus Christ. The apostles performed signs and wonders; the believers held all things in common, distributing their goods to those in need; they prayed in the Temple and broke bread in their homes, continually praising and thanking God for all things.

This was the remarkable beginning of the Christian Church. It did not begin with a new doctrine or theory. It began with a remembrance of the life, death and resurrection of Jesus, and with the wind and fire of God, sweeping through human lives and changing them for ever. The Spirit of God may give gifts of prophecy (preaching or speech inspired by God), wisdom and understanding, healing, and ecstatic speech in tongues (1 Corinthians 12.8–10, 28–31). Paul ranks them in this order, though he mentions other gifts – of leadership, ministry, and above all, the 'theological virtues' of faith, hope and love – 'and the greatest of these is love' (1 Corinthians 13.13).

The Christian life is a life possessed and changed by the divine Spirit. It may manifest remarkable gifts of healing and liberating power, or divinely inspired speech and insight, as with the prophets of ancient Israel and Judah. But each Spirit-guided life, however apparently unremarkable, possesses even greater qualities: 'the fruit of the Spirit is love, joy, peace, patience, kindness, generosity, faithfulness, gentleness, and self-control' (Galatians 5.22).

At the festival of Pentecost Israel remembered the giving of God's Law at Sinai. At this new Pentecost, Jesus' disciples came to see that 'if you are led by the Spirit, you are not subject to the law' (Galatians 5.18). There is a new law for the Church, the 'law of Christ': not a written code, but a law written on the heart (Jeremiah 31.33–34), and not a set of rules, but an inwardly guiding personal presence. The Spirit of Christ begins to conform the heart to the pattern of Christ, and to incorporate it into the life of God, until the day when, with face unveiled, we shall see Christ as he is.

22
The Gospel of John

The Gospel of John is so different in style and content from the other three Gospels that it calls for separate consideration. It begins with a clear affirmation that Jesus is the incarnation, the embodiment in human form, of the eternal Word, the Logos, of God. The word *logos* means word, intellect, reason or wisdom. It was used by the Jewish writer Philo of Alexandria to denote the wisdom of God which is Torah, the teaching by God of the way to human fulfilment. It is also what we might call the archetype or pattern of all creation, the blueprint in the mind of God for what creation is and should be. These elements are closely connected, for human fulfilment is to be attained by embodying that blueprint on the planet earth.

There was always a sense in which the *logos* was to be fully realized in the future, as humans played their part in shaping the cosmos towards its intended goal. But through selfish desire, hatred and self-deceit, human life had departed very far from the path to the goal. The path itself had become obscured and corrupted. Laws that were meant for good had become means of oppression and hypocrisy, and any sense of the presence of God had become dim and fitful.

In this world, says John, 'the Word became flesh' (John 1.14). The wisdom of God was fully realized in a particular human life. It is from this perspective that the Gospel of John is written. It does not attempt to provide an exact historical record. It seeks to present the meaning of Jesus' life and teachings by putting explicit explanations of that meaning into the mouth of Jesus. In the Synoptic Gospels, Jesus teaches in short, cryptic parables, and forbids the disciples to say publicly that he is the Messiah – and that is likely to reflect the historical reality. In John, Jesus gives a series of long speeches; and he explicitly declares that he is the bread of life upon which his disciples must feed (John 6.35), the light of the world by which they must be illumined (8.12), the true vine of which his disciples are the branches (15.1), the good shepherd (10.11), the resurrection and the life (11.25), the way, the truth and the life (14.6), one who existed before Abraham (8.58), and who is the only way to eternal life (14.6).

The focus of attention has shifted away from obedience to Torah and the pursuit of true righteousness, to participation in the eternal wisdom of God, fully expressed in Jesus and made present by the Holy Spirit, the Paraclete or Advocate. There is very little, if any, emphasis on the imminent coming of the kingdom of God, in which Jesus and the apostles will rule the reunited tribes of Israel in Jerusalem. Instead, the person of Jesus itself becomes the central focus, and Jesus is important because he is the embodied Life, Wisdom, and Light of God, in whose risen life all can share, and without whom the world remains a realm of death, ignorance and darkness.

This is recognizably the same Jesus as in the Synoptics: healing, preaching, attracting disciples, claiming virtually divine authority and uniquely close knowledge of God as Father, arousing the opposition of the religious establishment, being killed by men and being raised to new life by God. But John has read back into Jesus' historical life the early Church's experience of his resurrection life. Jesus becomes the one in and through whom the Word of God dispels the darkness of the world, and raises humans to participate in the divine life. What is implicit and hidden in the Synoptics becomes explicit and open in John. The cryptic parables of the kingdom are transformed into overt declarations of the incarnation of the eternal in time.

John's Gospel provides the vital key to interpreting the pictures of the coming kingdom that are drawn in the Synoptic Gospels. If John is right, these are not literal predictions of a sudden end to history, the instantaneous overthrow of the Roman Empire, and the visible triumph of the nation of Israel. They are symbolic ways of speaking of a more hidden, spiritual truth – the entrance, in and through the person of Jesus, of the eternal into time and the genesis of a new and primarily inward society of the Spirit.

We enter the kingdom as we share in the new life of Christ. The judgement is that, if we do not share in that life as it draws near to us, we remain in darkness ('This is the judgement, that the light has come into the world, and the people loved darkness rather than light', John 3.19). This should not be misunderstood as saying that all who do not explicitly believe in Christ will be condemned eternally. The one who is the only way to eternal life is the eternal Word. That Word is fully manifested in Jesus, but its presence is not confined to Jesus – it is the 'true light which enlightens everyone' (John 1.9). What we see in Jesus is the nature of God's Wisdom, but that Wisdom is the pattern of all creation, and is present to sustain the whole cosmos in every part, and illumines every human heart that is open to it.

That is why Christ does not condemn us: 'God did not send the Son into the world to condemn the world' (John 3.17). We condemn ourselves by our preference for darkness. But if and when we turn to the light, then we will be transformed by it. There is no point beyond which it is impossible for us to turn, and there is no place where the light is unable to shine. John's gospel is that if we follow the light, where and when we see it, in the end we will come to know that the true light is the eternal Son, who was and is embodied in Jesus the Christ, and is known in the community of the Church that is now his earthly body.

To be a disciple of Jesus is to share, through his Spirit, in the very life of God. Perhaps, the Synoptic Gospels suggest, Jesus could not say that during his ministry in Galilee. But perhaps that is, after all, the deepest secret of the parables of the kingdom.

The early development of doctrine

23
The gospel of the apostles

The gospel that both Paul and the apostles preached was not about detailed events in the life of Jesus, or primarily about his teachings. Usually delivered to people who had never known Jesus, it proclaimed five simple things: Jesus was the Righteous One, the promised Messiah (or, for non-Jews, the Saviour from evil). He had been wrongly killed. But he had risen from death and had been seen by the apostles. He would return to judge the world. Now, as a spiritual presence, he forgives sins and pours out the Spirit of God on all who repent and trust in him.

This was not primarily a new doctrine or moral code. It was a testimony to the liberation from sin ('salvation') and newness of life in the divine Spirit that the apostles had experienced. This testimony assumed the God of historic Judaism, creator and judge of all the world. But it spoke of a new, more inward covenant, an experience of life in the Spirit, a new birth. And it rapidly broke the bounds of Messianic Judaism and became a covenant open to all people, Jew and Gentile alike.

In the early Church, two main ceremonies marked out the Christian path. Baptism expressed a new birth into the society of the new covenant, a participation in the life of the risen Christ. And the 'breaking of bread' continued this participation, as the disciples celebrated the continuing presence of Christ among them, and sought to be filled with his life, dying to the egoistic self and being raised to share the life of God.

These were not realities alien to Judaism. The disciples of Jesus saw them as an authentic fulfilment of the Jewish traditions of covenant and 'marriage' to God ('As the bridegroom rejoices over the bride, so shall your God rejoice over you': Isaiah 62.5). But most Jews did not accept that Jesus was the Messiah – after all, the militaristic power of Rome had not been overthrown, and Israel had not triumphed. And the proclamation of Jesus as the channel of the life of God, saviour from evil and from divine judgement, attracted large numbers of Gentiles. A parting from historic Judaism became inevitable.

The book of Acts, chapter 15, records the first Church council, in Jerusalem, at which the apostles, now leaders of the new church, agreed to exempt Gentile converts from obedience to the full Torah. This was the second decisive move in the formation of a distinctively Christian Church. The first was the reinterpretation of the idea of Messiah from that of nationalistic liberator to a spiritual liberator from egoistic desire. This move from public and external to hidden and inward liberation was necessary if Jesus was truly to be acknowledged as Messiah.

Yet at the time the New Testament documents were written, the move was incomplete. Some still expected a public and visible return of Jesus in judgement in the near future. The spiritualization of this belief is, as John's Gospel puts it, that 'the light has come into the world, and people loved darkness rather than light' (John 3.19). Judgement is not a future public event. It is the choice of the heart for light or darkness. The condemnation is to live in darkness, a darkness that leads to spiritual death. Vindication (and the Holy Spirit is the Paraclete: Advocate or Vindicator) is to live in the light of God, a light that gives eternal life. Nor is this just a present spiritual reality. There will be a future in which each of us will have to face up to what we have made of our lives, and in which the Wisdom of God who was truly seen in Jesus will make clear to us the path we may have chosen that leads to death, but will still offer life to all who turn from evil. That is the 'return' of Jesus in judgement, and the gospel call is to receive the gift of life now, before our hearts grow harder and the turning grows more difficult.

If the first Christian revolution was to spiritualize the expectation of the Messiah, the second was to spiritualize the requirement of obedience to Torah. Jesus had taught that the Law should be kept in detail (Matthew 5.18), but had stressed that it should be interpreted in a humane way, and that sincerity of heart was more important than mere external observance. He was then speaking to Jews, however, and as Paul preached to Gentiles, the question arose as to whether they too should become observant Jews.

The apostles disagreed about this, James (the brother of Jesus) sending colleagues out to new churches to insist on observance (Galatians 2.11–14). Paul argued that new spiritual freedom in Christ entailed freedom from all written Law. And Peter had a three-fold vision which convinced him that Gentiles were not bound by at least the ritual prescriptions of the Law (Acts 10.28). At the first council, after much discussion, it was decided that Gentiles need not keep all the Law (though kosher food laws remained partly in place).

This move too was incomplete. It was not long (though after the writing of the New Testament) before the food laws were also dropped by the Church, and at that point Christianity became a non-Jewish faith. This was a momentous decision for the Church. It had some very bad consequences, since it helped to lead to the anti-Jewish thought which has disfigured the Church for much of its history. But it also had other implications. Christianity became a religion without a revealed written or oral Law. The Wisdom of God was enshrined, not in a text, but in the person of Jesus, the Word of God. Even the recorded words of the historical Jesus were held not to be binding on believers if there was good reason to adapt them to different circumstances (so his teaching to Jews was modified for Gentile believers). And in Paul's letters Christ is presented as 'the end of the Law' (Romans 10.4) – that is, both its fulfilment and its cessation.

Henceforth, Christians should seek to have 'the mind of Christ' (1 Corinthians 2.16), but that mind is not fossilized in some written text or set of unchangeable rules. It is a mind of self-giving, limitless compassion and companionship, a mind and heart of love. That mind is not learned by obedience to rules, but by openness to the Spirit of God, whose fruits in human minds are peace, patience, joy, kindness, gentleness and compassion (Galatians 5.22).

This is a message so radical that the Church has often not been able to bear it, and has insisted on obedience to rules as a condition of faith. That message does indeed have the danger that people may misuse their freedom badly, and there is evidence that some early Christians did that, indulging in orgies and drinking bouts.

The Law, then, should not simply be abandoned. It must be seen to be fulfilled in Christian life. Christians must seek discernment, to see the inner principles which underlie external rules, and to see the way in which Jesus' compassion points to a more humane redrawing of some biblical rules, or to their revision in the light of the more fundamental principles expressed in the Sermon on the Mount and in Jesus' compassion, humility and death.

The gospel preached by the apostles is thus centred on the person of Jesus, but not on the details of his past life or teaching. It is centred on the risen presence of the Saviour who gave his life in order that God's purposes might not fail, who liberates from the power and despair of sin those who turn to him, who communicates the divine life to them, and promises them the fulfilment of their lives in God. The gospel of Christ flourished because it was a gospel of new and more abundant life in a world so often filled with hatred and destruction. That gospel is as necessary now as it was then, and its relevance has not diminished with the passing of time.

24

Incarnation

As the early Church reflected on the role of Jesus in bringing to it a new knowledge of God, it wrestled with the question of the relationship between Jesus the man and God the creator. For some the impact of his life and personality was such that they believed him to be more than human, to be a human appearance of God in person, master of the physical and spiritual worlds, clothed for a time in human form. But others were more aware that Jesus was truly human, with all the limitations that are inseparable from humanity, though his whole life seemed to mediate an address from God to the human world.

It was not until the Council of Chalcedon, in AD 451, that what became the orthodox doctrine was finally formulated, that Jesus was both fully human and fully divine, two natures united in one person or *hypostasis*. Some have claimed that this is a contradiction. How could Jesus both be mortal (as man) and immortal (as God), limited in power and knowledge (as man) yet omnipotent and omniscient (as God)? But the orthodox view is quite consistent in holding that two different sets of powers can be united in one reality, without confusing them or bringing them into conflict. An analogy that was sometimes used by early theologians is that the body might be unconscious and subject to death, while the soul might be conscious and immortal. Yet the soul can be embodied, and form a unity in which body and soul are both essential to the full human reality.

This analogy might suggest, however, that Jesus had a human body but no human soul, his body being animated solely by his divine nature. That was an early view that the Third Council of Constantinople, in AD 680, finally ruled out. Jesus had a soul that was truly human and embodied. But that full human reality might form a unity of being with the creator of all things. Such a unity would not collapse one aspect into another, or confuse the human with the divine. But it would hold divine and human together in a unity that constitutes a distinctive form of reality. Thereafter, to speak of Jesus without speaking of the eternal Word, or to speak of the eternal Word without speaking of Jesus, would be to miss out a vital element of what each of them is. For Jesus is humanity-united-to-the-eternal-Word, and the Word is the-Word-united-to-humanity-in-Jesus.

Such a unity is contingent, in that the Word might not have become incarnate, or Jesus might not have been one with the Word. Yet it is a real unity – as the First Council of Nicaea, in AD 325, put it, Jesus is 'of one being' (*homoousion*) with God, not just 'like' God. To be like God is to imitate some divine properties, and all humans are like God in potentially having wisdom, understanding, compassion and freedom. But to be 'one' with God is to have the centre of one's self enfolded in the self of God, in such a way that one cannot fall away, and there is the deepest interpenetration of human and divine.

We might think of two wills, each with their own source of creative action, yet so linked that one would never act without the knowledge and consent of the other, and each would fully share with the other all their intentions and experiences. This would be a unity of separate wills, in which each will is changed by their union, and they could not exist apart without losing something of their innermost selves. We might further think that such a union is not a merging of two wills that were originally distinct. It is a union that binds the wills together from the first, so that one does not ever act without the other.

We might think of incarnation as an original and indissoluble union of divine and human wills. In a divine–human union, however, the divine must take priority. The divine will has acted without the human, and it continues to act throughout the universe, far beyond the limits of any human will. The divine experience includes all possible knowledge, and far exceeds the capacity of any human mind. For this reason, there cannot be a complete exchange of knowledge and experience. The finite will may only know of God what is possible for a finite and embodied being. But it may nevertheless have an immediate and unimpaired knowledge of the mind of God that is uncorrupted by passion or by that cultural estrangement that has been called 'original sin'.

Similarly, the human will can never have the omnipotence of the divine will. Yet it will never have acted in separation from the divine will. It may be totally enfolded from the first in the divine will, without its proper capacity for creative action being destroyed. Indeed, its human power and creativity would be vastly increased by its total alignment with the divine power. If we think of incarnation in this way, as a perfect marriage of wills, divine and human, all thought of contradiction falls away.

Such a human will would not be morally free, in the sense of being able to rebel against the divine will. In that respect, Jesus is different from all other human beings. He is necessarily good and filled with the divine life from the first moment of his existence. But that does not make him less than human. On the contrary, it makes him the ideal towards which humans may strive. For it is the goal of human life to reach a sort of union with God from which it is impossible to fall away, and in which all our acts and experiences will be grounded in and in perfect synergy with God. In that sense, Jesus is the point in history at which we can discern the end of human history, the goal at which it aims. He is 'Son of God' by birth; we hope to be 'sons of God' by adoption.

The incarnation is a foreshadowing in history of the end of history. Moreover, if we accept the testimony of the apostles, Jesus is designated by God as the Messiah, the Davidic King who is the true icon of God in human history. As such he makes visible in history the reality, nature and purpose of the God who is beyond history. He is the fullest form of the manifestation of the eternal God in time. For this reason, we can properly worship God in and through the person of Jesus, for in him God is present in human form. Though the divine nature is invisible and beyond human understanding, in the person of Jesus God mediates that nature in a form we can know and revere. Thus in coming to know Jesus, insofar as we see him as the historical mediator of the infinite God, and without claiming that thereby we understand everything about God, we may properly say, with the apostle Thomas, 'My Lord and my God' (John 20.28).

25
The Trinity

Jesus, like all orthodox Jews, taught that 'the Lord our God, the Lord is one' (Mark 12.29). But as his followers came to believe that Jesus himself was the earthly image of the invisible creator, so they came to think that the one and only God, the wise creator of the cosmos, unbounded and omnipotent, could also exist in finite form. It was not that there were two gods, but that the one God could exist in more than one form. God could exist as the unlimited abyss of being, from which all finite beings and forms arise. But God could also exist as divine mind or wisdom, as Logos, having awareness of and appreciating and enjoying all possible things, ordering and evaluating them as objects in the divine consciousness. The followers of Jesus came to think that this cosmic Logos took human form in the person of Jesus. In him the divine mind had taken a perfect human form, without losing anything of the divine infinity.

Yet the Jesus of history had died and entered into the spiritual realm, being no longer present on earth. God continued to be present on earth, however, in a particular form – no longer the form of an individual human person, but an inner presence in the hearts of those who had discerned the divine life in Jesus of Nazareth.

According to John's Gospel, Jesus promised to send the Spirit, an advocate or vindicator (one who frees from condemnation and judgement), one who will guide us into the truth, who will declare the promises of God, who will be an inner light, and make God's covenant present as a reality, not on tablets of stone, but within the heart (John 14.15–26;

16.4–15). The Spirit is the particular presence of God in the minds and hearts of men and women, enabling them to continue Jesus' work of healing, reconciliation and forgiveness throughout human history. Through the Spirit, the pattern and reality of Jesus' life is repeated in the lives of millions of men and women, who continue to be, even if in a partial and imperfect way, the body of Christ, the embodiment of God, on earth.

The First Council of Constantinople, in AD 381, defined the Spirit as fully divine, and not just a finite spirit sent from God. It is God in person who dwells and works within the heart, not some lesser spiritual being or power. So God was seen to exist within the cosmos, not only as its unchanging creator, and not only as expressed in one particular finite form, but also as the creative and life-giving force potentially present within the lives of all finite persons, enabling them to share in the divine life.

At that point the three-fold form in which God is discerned by Christians was portrayed in its main outlines. God is Father, as unbounded creator of the cosmos. God is Son, as a particular finite manifestation of the divine wisdom. God is Spirit, as the life-giving presence of God at the centre of every finite personality, and perhaps of every sentient being, drawing all creation towards union with the divine life. God is indivisibly one, but the revelation of the divine nature in Jesus shows God to exist in three forms of being, primordial, expressive, and unitive, all present in every divine action, yet irreducible to one another.

The doctrine of the Trinity is not some abstract piece of speculation. It is based on the belief that in Jesus the eternal God is seen truly expressed in human form, and that the same Spirit who filled the life of Jesus also lives in human lives, uniting them to the divine life. The doctrine of the Trinity reveals that God enters into human life, sharing human joys and sorrows, and that finite lives are taken into the eternal being of God, to become 'participants in the divine nature' (2 Peter 1.4). The Trinitarian God is a God who unites divine and human, first in Christ, then in those who die to self in order to live in Christ, and ultimately in a wholly renewed and divinized creation. Thus the Trinity is at the heart of the Christian gospel, the good news that all can be released from the bondage of the self and liberated into the freedom of life in God.

26

Atonement

'Without the shedding of blood there is no forgiveness of sins . . . Jesus has appeared once for all at the end of the age to remove sin by the sacrifice of himself' (Hebrews 9.22, 26). Jesus is the finite expression of the divine, the human 'image of the invisible God' (Colossians 1.15). But from the beginning it has been central to Christian faith to believe that Jesus is also the Saviour of the world, the High Priest who offers himself to take away the sin of the world. This is the atonement, the forgiveness of sin by the shedding of the blood of Jesus.

Sacrifice was at the heart of ancient Jewish Temple worship. In whole offerings and fellowship offerings, and in sin and guilt offerings, worshippers would take a perfect animal, lay their hands upon its head, and kill it as an offering to God. The meat would often be shared, but the fat and the blood belonged to God, because the fat is the best part of the meat, and because 'the life of every creature is its blood' (Leviticus 17.14). God said, 'I have given it [blood] to you for making atonement for your lives on the altar; for, as life, it is the blood that makes atonement' (Leviticus 17.11).

It is thus the offering of life that heals the breach between God and humans that some wrong act has caused. The life of an animal is offered in place of the wrongdoer's life. Sacrifices were costly – animals had to be perfect – and they can be seen as gifts given to God to restore an impaired relationship. God, of course, is not a highly sensitive soul who has to be appeased by small gifts. But the ritual of sacrifice is a human act that expresses sorrow, the desire to make amends, an element of self-renunciation, and preparedness to make a public and external symbolic act of offering one's own life to God.

The whole point of sacrifice is not to change God, but to express, in public and external ways, inner attitudes of repentance, renewed commitment, self-giving, adoration and gratitude. If that which has been offered to God is then shared (if one shares the meat, or is sprinkled with the sacrificial blood), this is a symbol that one now truly shares in life that has become divine, in God's own life.

For Christians, Jesus is in the unique position of not having to atone for any sin of his own, or to perform any ritual to unite his life to that of God. For his life is perfectly united to God from the first, and he is without sin. Yet his whole life is a perfect sacrifice, a perfect offering of self to God. The sacrifice of Jesus is not just his death. It is the total offering of his life. In a world estranged and alienated from God, such a God-filled life was bound to lead to persecution and death, as human hatred of goodness sought to eliminate all that threatens the rule of selfish desire (symbolized as the rule of Satan). Jesus' death epitomized the totality of his self-offering, but it is the offering of his life that is important. For through that human life totally offered to God, all that separates human from divine was removed, and Jesus became the medium by which the divine life flooded into the world with healing power.

In the Eucharist the sacrifice of Jesus is made present so that we can make it our own sacrificial offering to God. Receiving the body and blood of Christ, we can receive the divine life that sets aside the desiring self and replaces it with a self centred in God. This sacrifice and liberating power are definitively set forth, first in the life of Jesus, then in the sacrament of the Eucharist. But they are meant for the whole world, that it should be liberated from desire and united to God through the self-giving love of God that was definitively manifested in Jesus. This is what it means to say that human sin is expiated by the shedding of the blood of Jesus.

Three main metaphors of the atonement have been used in Christian tradition. One is the metaphor of 'ransom', used by the fourth-century theologian Gregory of Nyssa – 'the Son of Man came . . . to give his life a ransom for many' (Mark 10.45). Jesus liberates humans from slavery to self by offering his life as a ransom. Victory over the forces of evil is won, not by violence but by self-sacrifice. By sharing human suffering, God pays a price that liberates humans from the selfish desire that causes suffering.

Another is the metaphor of 'satisfaction', used in the eleventh century by Anselm, and in the sixteenth century in a rather different form by Luther and Calvin. We owe a debt that we can never pay, and Jesus pays it in our place. God does what we are unable to do, and frees us from the sentence of spiritual death that is the natural consequence of our desire-led lives. God in human form dies that we might live.

A third is the metaphor of 'healing', associated in the eleventh century with Peter Abelard and in the twentieth with Paul Tillich. The cross shows the extent of God's love for us, and if humans respond to that love, the Holy Spirit makes it effective in us, and releases a power of healing, of New Being, that makes human lives whole.

These and other metaphors drawn from various strands of the Bible are limited ways of pointing to the basic fact that 'God's love was revealed among us in this way: God sent his only Son into the world so that we might live through him . . . God sent his Son to be the atoning sacrifice for our sins' (1 John 4.9, 10). It is not that God had to send someone else to die because of what we had done, before God felt able to forgive us. The truth is that God in person took human form, and in that form shared in human suffering, surrendering his human life totally, in order that every barrier of self that stands between humanity and God should be broken down, and that we might live more abundantly by receiving the divine life and love that God gives. The doctrine of the atonement is the doctrine that God loved us so greatly that God entered into human suffering and death, so that we might be saved from spiritual death, and receive the gift of eternal life: 'I am convinced that neither death, nor life, nor angels, nor rulers, nor things present, nor things to come, nor powers, nor height, not depth, nor anything else in all creation, will be able to separate us from the love of God in Christ Jesus our Lord' (Romans 8.38–39).

27
The Church

The idea of the Church is distinctive to and definitive of Christianity. The Church is 'the body of Christ' (1 Corinthians 12.27). If a body is the means of expressing a personal reality in history, the vehicle of that person's actions in the world, and the local and identifiable presence of that person, then the Church expresses what Christ is, mediates the acts of Christ, and is the means by which Christ is present in the world, in a particular recognizable form.

Yet it is immediately clear that this is an ideal that is not fully realized in history. Whereas Jesus was fully united to the divine Logos from the first, and was without sin, the members of the Church are never wholly free of sin – of hatred, greed, ignorance and pride. So it might be true to say that the Church only wholly exists insofar as the Spirit of Christ truly lives and acts in the lives of its members, enabling them to express Christ appropriately, mediate the selflessly loving acts of Christ unconditionally, and bear the presence and image of Christ transparently in their minds (so that they know Christ inwardly), their hearts (so that they love Christ intensely), and their lives (so that they share Christ's passion and Christ's joy to the full).

This would only be possible if, and it will be possible when, we are liberated from sin. Now we live in a time of paradox, when we are still bound to sin, yet God calls us nonetheless to be Christ's body, to die to our sinful selves and share Christ's risen life. In other words, the Church now exists partially and imperfectly, but God promises that our life in Christ will reach completion, as the Spirit gradually yet inexorably liberates us and makes us whole. That is what salvation is, something that lies ahead in its fullness, yet has now begun as an active and irreversible power making for human fulfilment in God.

The present Church is the assurance that we shall be, clearly and consciously, members of the fellowship of the Spirit, united and fulfilled in Christ, and it is the means by which we begin to be in Christ at this present time. The Church genuinely exists wherever people take Jesus as their Lord, the finite human manifestation of the divine Logos; wherever they seek to let the Spirit that was in and sent by Jesus live and work in them; and wherever, responding to the life, death and resurrection of Jesus, they understand God's nature as unlimited love and God's purpose as being to raise all things to participate in the divine nature.

Many historic Christian churches have narrower views than this. The Roman Catholic Church claims that the Church fully exists only where there are bishops in a continuous line of succession from the apostles, where baptism incorporates people into the body of Christ, where the Eucharist is celebrated as a making-present of Jesus' sacrifice and a means of conveying his risen life to devotees, and where the divinely appointed leadership of the Pope is accepted.

The Orthodox churches regard papal supremacy as a post-apostolic innovation, but regard episcopacy and the reception of the sacraments of baptism and the Eucharist, described in the Gospels as instituted by Jesus himself, as essential for the Church.

Protestant churches usually regard episcopacy as just one possible development of patterns of Church leadership, and often say, as Calvin did, that the Church exists wherever the gospel is preached, and the sacraments of baptism and the Eucharist are celebrated by a community. The gospel is essential, for there must be reliable remembrance of Jesus, if he is to be the pattern and source of faith. The dominical sacraments are the biblically attested means by which people can die with Christ, in baptism, and receive the life of Christ in the Eucharist. This is in principle a more inclusive view of the Church, as the company of all who seek to know and love Christ, and let his risen life, through the Spirit whom he sends, transfigure them into the divine image.

The Roman Catholic and Orthodox traditions may be taken as natural developments from the primitive Christian churches, contributing invaluable resources for spirituality, doctrinal reflection and the richness of life in Christ. But from a Protestant point of view, they are developments, and would benefit from being open to a more inclusive view of the Church, and from a stronger emphasis on the ubiquity of human sin and the corruptibility of all social institutions.

Questions about what in detail the content of the gospel is, or about how and when the sacraments should be celebrated, will also on this wider view allow of a plurality of interpretations. Freedom of dissent and of belief, and acceptance of informed critical enquiry, are important elements of a liberal approach to Christian faith. Such a liberal approach will not lay down specific doctrines, whether radical or conservative, as mandatory. It will ask only that all sincerely continue to seek fuller truth, and accept the fact of conscientious diversity among those who believe in common that the cosmos is created by a God that wills the salvation of all, who take Jesus as the definitive revelation of God's nature and promises, and who seek to live by the inward power of the Spirit and to grow towards fullness of being in Christ.

On such a view, the Church will always be diverse in its forms and institutions. It will, ideally, be held together through bonds of friendship and common love of God in Christ. It will be one, as Jesus and the Father are one, united by bonds of love and mutual relationship. It will seek to be in the world as Jesus was, a reconciling, healing, forgiving, serving presence and witness to the unlimited love of God. It will confess its frailty, obtuseness, and liability to corruption. But it will maintain its distinctive claim that within its many forms of fellowship God acts to unite humanity, and through humanity the world, within the divine life.

That unity may often be obscured, or even sometimes almost lost. But God's promise is that it will not finally fail, and that on the rock of Peter's confession, 'You are the Christ, the Son of the Living God' (Matthew 16.16), such a fellowship will be founded that even the gates of Hades will not prevail against it.

Christianity in relation to the non-Christian world

28
Humanist values

If the Church is the promise and means of human salvation, what is to be said of the vast majority of human beings throughout history who have no connection with the Church?

The promise the Church gives is that God wills the salvation of all ('God our Saviour, who desires everyone to be saved', 1 Timothy 2.4). It follows that God must make salvation possible for all, and so the promise is not confined to the Church or to those who have heard the name of Jesus – though the Church shows what salvation is, and shows that salvation is possible for any person, in the Church or outside it.

Accordingly, the Church is the means of salvation, not as excluding all who are outside it, but as foreshadowing in time and imperfectly the way that all must finally take to come to the true God, whose nature is authentically disclosed in Jesus, and whose indwelling Spirit is truly given in the fellowship of Christ.

It is more important for the Church that it is called to be Christ in the world, to serve the world in love, not to condemn the world as outside the possibility of salvation (Jesus said, 'I came not to judge the world, but to save the world', John 12.47). So while the Church witnesses to what salvation truly is, and provides a divinely given way to salvation, it is also called to testify to the possibilities of salvation that God has created in the whole human world.

Salvation has two components – liberation from self and fulfilment by conscious union with the Supreme Good. The Supreme Good in turn has three main components – understanding of truth, the creation and appreciation of beauty, and that desire to share experience and action, to manifest open-hearted empathy and delight in others, that constitutes love.

Wherever in human life people turn from selfish desire towards truth, beauty and goodness, they take a step on the way to salvation. In the disinterested pursuit of scientific discovery, in devotion to music and art, in the selfless service of others, there is a turning away from self and towards God, the Supreme Good.

Such pursuits may be only fragmentary parts of worship, but they are nonetheless real. From a Christian viewpoint, any genuine search for truth is a turning towards the one who is Truth ('I am the way, and the truth, and the life', John 14.6). Any sensitivity to beauty is sensitivity to the one who is Supreme Beauty ('How beautiful you are, my love, how very beautiful', Song of Solomon 4.1). And any selfless regard for others is openness to the divine love ('God is love', 1 John 4.16). The One who is Truth, Beauty and Love may remain unrecognized and unconfessed, yet that One is present in every turning towards what is true and beautiful and good.

In the fullness of worship, the mind passes from particular truths to that which is alone truly real and self-existent, upon which all truths depend. It passes from particular beauties to that which is the source of all beauty and is itself the realized awareness of the supremely beautiful. It passes from particular acts of love to that which is the source of all goodness, which is supremely happy and self-realized, and which wills the happiness and fulfilment of all sentient beings.

This is the worship of God. It does not exclude any turning of the human mind towards the good, but seeks to unite and fulfil each turning to the good, however partial and imperfect, in a disclosure of the supreme objective Good that wills to draw all finite persons to conscious participation in its own comprehensive reality.

For Christians, the nature of the Supreme Good is disclosed in Jesus, the active power of the Supreme Good is felt in the inward presence of the Holy Spirit, and the promise of the Supreme Good is manifested in the resurrection of Jesus to the divine life. This does not limit salvation to those who believe these things. It shows what salvation is for all, and calls the Church to witness in its way of life to the fullness of salvation that will complete the way of all those who begin (even though they might never put it this way) to 'repent and believe', to turn their minds towards goodness in the faith that it truly exists and can be found.

The complication is that the Church will always fail in living out its calling. It may become an obstacle to faith by undue exclusiveness, hypocrisy, desire for power, or intolerance. After all, some religious leaders of God's covenant people conspired in the death of Jesus. Some leaders of Christian churches have similarly betrayed the message of Jesus, a message of tolerance, service and compassion.

The Church stands in constant need of forgiveness and renewal. For that reason it needs to be attentive to the perceptions of those who stand outside it, yet may contribute insights of their own to the Church's understanding of its true vocation, and to the as yet uncompleted fullness of the vision of Christ as universal saviour.

The Church in history has sometimes suppressed truth, censored the arts, and imposed restricted understandings of goodness. The critique made by humanism, a critique of religious repression and the suppression of human values and conscience in the name of blind acceptance of authority, has been a necessary part of Christian history. But humanism itself stands in need of the rational support that the affirmation of one supremely personal basis of reality can give. It is because humans are created in the image of the divine that they have a unique calling as morally responsible agents in the world. To affirm human values is not to oppose Christian faith. It is part of Christian faith. When the Church abandons its own calling, humanism can serve to remind the Church of what it should be. But the Church also serves to remind humanists that there is a fulfilment of human nature and values that is more sublime and expansive than anything humanism alone can offer. It is the fulfilment of human life in God, a universal destiny that adds a new depth and objectivity to the values of truth, beauty and love that humanists rightly celebrate.

29
Indian religious traditions

If God has never been absent from human life and experience, and if God is especially present in experiences of truth, beauty and goodness, we might expect that as humans seek to respond to spiritual reality, they are in fact responding to a God who in some way evokes and guides their spiritual quest.

Anthropological studies suggest that most pre-literate cultures accept a world of spirits, apprehended in visions, dreams and trances, and of holy persons who have special access to that world. There is a sense of a spiritual reality, but it seems to be pluriform, morally ambiguous, and depicted not in doctrines but in many different stories and rituals. The idea of one creator Spirit, concerned primarily with moral goodness, seems to be a rather late one, propounded in particular by the prophets of the Hebrews.

In other cultures, and particularly in India and China, ideas of spiritual reality developed in rather different ways. It was natural in the infancy of the human race to see spiritual reality as pluriform, as embodied in many different aspects of the experienced world. In India the many gods express the many aspects of the natural world and of the human mind. There are gods of sun and moon, of storm and thunder, of mountain and sea. There are gods of love and of hate, of revenge and of forgiveness, of moral law and of chance and luck.

As Indian religious thought developed, all these gods or spiritual powers came to be seen as aspects of one underlying spiritual reality, Brahman or Absolute Spirit. The shamans or holy men and women who 'saw' the spirits in dreams and visions, and who 'heard' their words in ecstatic trances, came to be seen as liberated souls who pierced the veil of illusion and intuited Absolute Spirit itself, in one of its many names and forms.

The Hebrew prophets thought of the one God as excluding the many gods, and of God as having a moral purpose for history. But in India the *rishis* or teachers thought of the one Brahman as including all the gods as aspects of itself, and of Spirit as being beyond all action and purpose. This world was seen as the realm of *maya*, a world created by desire and ruled by the law of karma, according to which all finite beings receive the rewards of their deeds for good or ill. In successive rebirths, creatures take many forms, but they are always to some extent under the sway of ignorance and desire, ignorance of their true spiritual nature and desire that traps them in attachment and egoism.

The spiritual goal is to achieve *moksa*, release from the wheel of rebirth. So there is no true purpose or goal in material existence itself. The object of human life is return to the One, and leave for ever the world of suffering and desire, attaining union with the Self of All, rooted in consciousness and bliss, unchanging, serene and beyond all action that is founded on restless desire.

As anyone who knows India would expect, matters are rather more complex than this may suggest. Gautama Buddha, the Enlightened One, was an Indian world-renouncer, and according to the Theravada tradition ('the ancient teaching'), he taught that belief in gods was not religiously important. The fact that the world is filled with suffering means that it cannot have been created by a benevolent God. It cannot even be the appearance of Absolute Spirit, for there is no substantial spirit, either in the cosmos or in the human body. What is important is to obtain release from the suffering that inevitably results from attachment to the world and selfish desires. Such release can be obtained by cultivating mindfulness and compassion, by the cessation of desire, and by non-attachment. It can be obtained by overcoming the illusion of being a separate substantial self, and realizing that one is a bundle of sensations, thoughts and feelings, held together by the illusion of a continuing self, and by desire. When release is obtained, one enters into Nirvana, a state beyond self and individuality and desire, yet having the nature of knowledge, compassion and bliss.

At the other extreme of the complex of Indian traditions, Brahman truly takes form as a supreme personal Lord, Isvara. By devotion to the Lord (often conceived in the form of Krishna, one of the *avatara* or finite manifestations of the supreme Lord), human souls can be liberated from earthly existence. But they continue to exist as spiritual individuals in a heavenly realm, where they love and serve the Lord in everlasting bliss.

It is not hard to see how God can be found in these Indian traditions, even when, as in Buddhism, God is overtly denied. For there is a search for liberation from evil. There is a desire to attain a state of wisdom, compassion and bliss. There is a stress on the necessity of cultivating universal compassion and overcoming selfish desire. And there is a belief that there is a basic moral order in the cosmos, and a higher and more desirable form of existence beyond this life.

Most Christians would emphasize the possibility of conscious relation to a personal God, and the need for an active divine initiative to liberate them from evil. They would doubt that we are reborn many times, and will finally lose our sense of individual identity. And they might want a more socially active sense of liberation and a more positive sense of a goal for the world than exists in Buddhism or in most forms of Hinduism.

Yet Christians might also find a profound conception of God in the idea of the Supreme Self of All, of whom all things are parts, or even in the Buddhist notion of a reality beyond all thought that has the nature of wisdom, compassion and bliss. They might find in the idea of compassion for all sentient beings a morality more extensive and inclusive than has often been found in their own faith. They might find in the emphasis on meditation and self-discipline a more practical means of spiritual training than they have been accustomed to. And they might find in the Indian teaching of infinitely many worlds, of the possibility of universal liberation, and of a positive evaluation of humans as parts, along with all other beings, of the body of God, a less judgemental and arrogant view of human existence and destiny.

So Christians can see the Indian traditions as guided by God towards more profound and inclusive perspectives, but as developing different basic metaphors for picturing human life in its relation to a supreme spiritual reality, metaphors not of a supreme Moral Will, but of an all-including Cosmic Self or an impersonal and unpicturable reality of knowledge, compassion and bliss.

We cannot yet see how these perspectives might in future intertwine or meet or co-exist. But there are good grounds for claiming that the different spiritual paths of humanity are differing approaches to a common spiritual goal that none of the traditions grasps with total adequacy. They are diverse forms of the interaction of divine inspiration and the culturally and historically formed creativity of the human imagination.

Christians can rejoice that the God of unlimited love revealed in and through Jesus is known in different forms in the religious traditions of India. At key points, the Christian tradition will seem to them to convey distinctive and important emphases and insights that should not be lost. But there is much that they can gratefully receive from traditions different from their own, that can help to fill out the global revelation of the nature and purpose of God in the whole pattern of human history. It may be that the Indian traditions contain insights that will be necessary to a deeper understanding of the Christian revelation itself.

30
East Asian religious traditions

In China and East Asia, religious belief and practice developed in a different way. The idea of one personal creator God was not an important feature of these traditions. What developed were forms of transcendental humanism – the main emphasis was on living a good and fulfilling human life. Such a life was felt to be a life in harmony with the inner structure of the cosmos, with what was sometimes called 'the Way of Heaven'.

Early religion had been concerned with human good and harm, and the spirits were consulted to help avoid harm and bring good, whether fertility, abundant harvest, or victory in war. In the Middle East and in India, attention concentrated on the nature of these spirits, and ideas of a dominant God or Absolute Spirit developed. But in China, attention focused on human good and harm. The transcendent dimension was not lost, but it was largely seen as a dimension of this present world in which humans live, not as a distinct or separate reality that is complete in itself.

In Taoism humans were counselled to live in harmony with the flow of nature, with the balanced forces of yin and yang. Human flourishing was to be found in harmony with the natural force that flows through all things. In Confucianism, on the other hand, human flourishing was found in obeying the social rules that preserved and reflected the Way of Heaven, the morally ordered life of courtesy, kindness and practical wisdom that was written into the law of human nature.

In both cases, underlying the seeming chaos of the natural world there was felt to be a moral order to which humans should conform if they were to find true fulfilment. Heaven (Tian) may not be a personal spirit or a separate state, but it underlies and gives moral order to the cosmos and to human life. There is a way in which humans ought to live, and this way is written objectively into the basic nature of the cosmos. There are beliefs in the continued existence of ancestors, in spirits and ghosts, but they never came to form a systematic and rationally articulated worldview. Rather, people seek the spiritual dimension in nature and in social relationships, and aim to relate to it by conforming their lives to its fundamental principles.

When Buddhism came to China (and was at one time its official religion), its main forms adopted this general outlook, and commended living in the world with mindfulness and non-attachment, rather than complete renunciation of the world. Nirvana was not seen as a separate state, but as this very world, seen with the eyes of enlightenment. The world of attachment and desire is a world of suffering and loss. But when the world is seen without attachment, it appears as it truly is, a shining flow of appearances whose true character is apprehended by a non-conceptual and non-dual pure awareness. Egoism falls away when it is seen that in reality there exists no enduring self to which to be attached. When one sees no ultimate difference between oneself and others, there remains no reason to seek one's own good in preference to that of others. Happiness in the unity of all beings is the natural result, as is compassion for those still lost in the ignorance of the desiring self.

This thought in East Asian and Chinese Buddhist traditions gives rise to the idea of the *bodhisattva*, an enlightened being who defers full enlightenment out of compassion for all sentient beings, that he may help them on the path to enlightenment. A *bodhisattva* may take a vow to renounce full enlightenment until all sentient beings obtain release from suffering. There are endless numbers of *bodhisattvas*, each having the nature of pure and compassionate mind, and for some Buddhist sects (like the 'Pure Land' movement) humans live in a world formed by such a being, and are destined, perhaps by devotion to the saviour-Buddha as well as by personal purification, for worlds of pure bliss in which the *bodhisattva* rules. At this point Christianity and Buddhism come remarkably close.

There are many forms of Chinese religion, but they all tend to stress the importance of enlightenment in this life, of compassion for all beings as a basic virtue, and of religious practice as a training in qualities of mind and will that conduces to joy, wisdom, kindness, and an insight into the nature of reality that is beyond conceptual description.

From such a religious viewpoint, the Semitic concern with one anthropomorphic God seems too literalistically naive. The Christian doctrine of sin, judgement and hell seems unduly gloomy and negative in its assessment of human nature. And Christian belief in one saviour who dies once on the cross to save those who call on his name is seen as much too limited and tortured a view of the nature of spiritual reality. After all, there are innumerable happy and serene Buddhas in innumerable worlds, who have compassion on all sentient beings. And though this world is a realm of suffering, it is also a realm in which there are many pathways for all to endless joy.

These views may seem a challenge to the ethical monotheism of the Semitic faiths, and they do challenge the literal, judgemental and exclusive beliefs that some Christians have held. But the Christian God is not at all anthropomorphic. Sin is just what Buddhists perceive as selfish desire, which has as its consequence suffering and spiritual death. Christ died for all, and his compassion for the world led him to share its sufferings. Nevertheless these Christian truths can be presented in ways which seem to restrict salvation to Christians only, and to lack any genuine concern for other sentient beings.

Perhaps East Asian approaches to religion are best seen by Christians as presenting a complementary perspective on spirituality. They miss the vision of a personal God who shares in the suffering of the world in order to offer all humans a share in the happiness and fulfilment of the divine love. But they witness to the importance of human fulfilment by liberation from a false sense of self and the cultivation of universal compassion and the simple enjoyment of being.

It should be remembered, too, that Heaven, the Tao or 'true way', and Nirvana are all spiritual (non-material) aspects of reality that are more than simply human or natural, and that set a supreme goal for human life. A Christian will see here the presence of God, drawing human lives towards that openness to divine love that will eventually reveal full participation in the personal love of God to be the goal of all finite beings.

God truly works in many ways to draw creation into the divine life. Christians naturally believe that in Jesus Christ a disclosure of that goal, as it truly will be, has been authentically given. That disclosure should never be used as a means of condemning or excluding others. For the Christian gospel is the offer of life and love to all, as the fulfilment of all inadequate human understandings. Many Christian understandings, too, will need to be expanded and renewed before the depths of revelation in Christ are plumbed. The East Asian religions may well have a positive part to play in allowing us to journey further into the mystery of Christ. But Christians may reasonably believe that the mystery of Christ is the final goal of every authentic religious journey, and that the Spirit of Christ is present in a thousand forms and faces, drawing human minds and hearts patiently but surely towards that goal.

31
Islam

It is not hard to see how Christ can be seen as the fulfilment of many hopes of the Old Testament. This carries dangers for Christian relations to Judaism, if Christians claim that their faith has superseded Judaism and rendered it obsolete. But I have suggested that it is possible, and preferable, to see Christianity as an offering of the fundamentals of the Jewish prophetic vision to the whole world, in a new form, while Jews are to remain loyal to their own special covenant with God.

Islam, however, is a more difficult case. Like Christianity and Judaism, it claims spiritual descent from Abraham and the prophets. But the prophet Muhammad is seen as the 'seal of the prophets', who corrects various mistakes that Jews and Christians have made, and recites the final and definitive words of God to humanity, the Qur'an. The Qur'an specifically forbids referring to Jesus as 'Son of God', and speaking of God as 'three'. It seems to deny that Jesus died on the cross (he ascended directly to heaven), and it restores a divine law (*shari'ah*) very like the Torah, but meant for all human beings.

Because Islam came into being as a distinct religion centuries after Christ, it is unreasonable to see Christ as its 'fulfilment', in any plausible sense. Islam denies the divinity of Christ and the mission of the Church. In addition, Christianity became the official faith of the Roman Empire, while Islam became the religion of various imperial powers, from the Arabs to the Mongols, the Moroccans and the Turks, who came into military conflict with the dying Roman Empire and the rising post-Roman powers of Europe.

These things have been a cause of regrettable hostility between the two great missionary world faiths, sprung from the same spiritual root, having similar entanglements with aggressive military powers, expanding successfully throughout the whole world, and occasionally each expressing the desire to dominate the whole world.

One way to blunt the edge of centuries of hostility is for Christians to think of Muslims as unitarians, who deny the Incarnation and the Trinity, but have great respect for Jesus and worship the same God of Abraham and the prophets. Christians can see how people can honestly find the doctrine that Jesus was divine impossible to understand, and think that somehow it wrongly confuses divine and human. Many Christians themselves find the doctrine of the Trinity difficult to understand, and it may seem simpler just to say, as Jesus did, 'the Lord our God, the Lord is one' (Mark 12.29).

Basically, Muslims believe in one creator God of justice, compassion and mercy, who will be the Judge of all people, and who will have mercy on all who turn to God. There is no church, there are no priests, no sacraments, no doctrine of original guilt and sin, and no need for a saviour, other than God, who has the power to bring all people to Paradise (and who, according to a well-attested tradition claiming to go back to the Prophet, will do so).

This is surely a simple and attractive faith, and Christians can understand that it could be seen as a return to the basics of faith in God, for people who cannot bear the complications of Christian doctrine, the hierarchical structures of the Church, and all the quarrels about abstruse dogmas that seem beyond logical resolution.

As for *shari'ah*, like Torah the Qur'an sets out a number of case-laws that need to be interpreted in later situations, and in the light of changing circumstances. As in Judaism, there is not just one way of interpreting the law, and scholars cover a whole spectrum of views, from attempts to take it fairly literally where possible and cover the whole of social and political life, to the acceptance that it is usually confined to religious and family matters, and says little directly about most of the major political and moral problems of our world.

Again the situation is complicated by the fact that many Muslim countries are extremely traditional, and impose traditions like the veiling of women or their confinement to the home that are not mentioned in the Qur'an. There are also Marxist-influenced movements in Islam, like the Muslim Brotherhood, that think terrorism is an acceptable response to alleged Western-backed attacks on Palestine and support of repressive political regimes in Muslim countries.

Christians need to remember that there have been Christian groups that have had similar views, that have tried to interpret biblical rules literally and enforce them socially, that have regarded women as subservient to men, and that have defended the use of violence, for example in the burning of heretics, and the papal blessing of the First Crusade in AD 1095.

Very few Christians would now defend these causes, and there are very many Muslims who would be equally critical of violent and ultra-conservative interpretations of Islam. So there is much room for the development of further understanding between Islam and Christianity, neither of which, as history clearly shows, are monolithic and unchanging entities. Christians will not be able to accept that the Qur'an is the actual words of God without human interpretation or error, since it includes what they would regard as legendary material about the childhood of Jesus, denies the incarnation and the Trinity, and regards Muhammad as correcting the teaching of the New Testament. In this respect, both Christians and Muslims must think that the scripture of the other group contains some errors. But Christians can accept that the Qur'an is a remarkable work truly inspired by God, teaching the sovereignty of God, the truth of divine judgement, the certainty of divine mercy, and the promise of life with God for all who strive to obey and love God. Christians can accept Muhammad as a prophet and a remarkable spiritual leader, who, being in a different context from that of Jesus, was able to show how social and political leadership could be discharged with complete devotion to God. And Christians can accept Islam as a worldwide community of obedience to God's law of social justice, which can co-operate with the Christian Church in seeking such justice, and in seeking to implement it with humane and universal love.

The case of Islam acts as a reminder to Christians that we sometimes make our faith needlessly complicated, and attempt to confine God's activity too much to our Church institutions. Yet the central Christian good news is that God has entered into both the joys and the sufferings of the human situation. God has united human nature in the most intimate possible way to the divine nature in Jesus. God intends the Church to be the means whereby the divine Spirit acts inwardly in human lives to unite us all to the divine nature in Christ. And God intends that all creation should become a sacrament of the divine presence, truly revealed as unlimited self-giving love in Jesus.

Christians have the responsibility to proclaim this good news throughout the world, and to do so with love, tolerance and sensitivity. The Christian witness must always be the witness of a love that serves others, and that does not seek to impose its views by force. The freedom of Muslims, like that of other non-Christians, to worship God conscientiously must be protected. God will draw to the divine life all whom God wishes, in the ways God wishes. For truth, and the way to truth, belong to God and not to us.

Defining moments in Christian history

―――――•◆•―――――

32
Martyrs, icons and monks

Christianity began among a group of Jews who were convinced that Jesus was the promised Messiah, a belief confirmed by his appearances to a group of disciples after his death, and by their experience of the Holy Spirit filling them with a vital sense of Christ's continuing presence with them. This early group, the 'Church' or congregation of believers, was led by the twelve apostles, originally appointed by Jesus to preach and heal in Judaea, but becoming witnesses who had known Jesus and could testify to his resurrection.

At first the Church spread rapidly among the Jews, but especially under the influence of Paul, it attracted many Gentile converts, and in a short while became a predominantly Gentile community, eventually splitting away from Judaism altogether, as the Torah was abandoned, the Jewish priesthood was abolished with the destruction of the Temple in AD 70, and Christians saw themselves as a community of a 'new covenant' with God. Centring their worship of God on the person of Jesus, they sought to die with Christ to the world of egoism and greed, live in the power of his resurrection life, and look for the fulfilment of all things when Christ would appear in glory to bring history to its end.

For the first three hundred years the Church expanded around the Mediterranean coasts, mostly in territories belonging to the Roman Empire. Christians suffered sporadic persecution from the Roman authorities, particularly under the emperors Nero, Decius and Diocletian. 'The blood of the martyrs is the seed of the Church', wrote Tertullian, and thousands of Christians went to their deaths for refusing to worship the Emperor or the deities of the Roman pantheon as gods, and for their undivided loyalty to Christ alone. Their care for one another, for the poor and the sick, was legendary, and the Church continued to grow as followers of Christ showed by their deaths their faithfulness to a God of love rather than to the gods of power and wealth. As Jesus himself died for the sake of a love that is stronger than death, so many of his disciples, including many apostles, gave their lives for the sake of a beauty beyond all earthly beauties, and a love beyond all earthly loves, suffering bodily death to share with their Saviour a spiritual and eternal life.

Perhaps the most decisive and dramatic change in Christian history occurred when, almost a century after the conversion of the Emperor

Constantine to Christianity, it became the official religion of the Roman Empire in AD 395. Constantine founded 'New Rome', Constantinople, in AD 330, and took up residence there. By 395 the Roman Empire had decisively divided into the Eastern (Byzantine) Empire and the Western (Latin) Empire. The Church in its new imperial role became a more formalized and hierarchical institution, presided over by five patriarchates – Jerusalem, Constantinople, Rome, Alexandria and Antioch. Rome, by tradition the place where Paul and Peter had died, held primacy of honour, but Constantinople, capital of Byzantium, claimed primacy over the Eastern Church, and each Patriarch had jurisdiction in their own areas. It was in and around Constantinople that the first ecumenical councils of the Church were held, councils that defined what became the orthodox doctrines that Jesus was fully human and fully divine, and that the Trinity was a union of Father, Son and Spirit in one divine being.

The seventh and last ecumenical council, at Nicaea in AD 787, decreed that icons could be properly reverenced, and was meant to end a long controversy about whether images of Jesus and the saints were permissible. It was not, however, until 843 that arguments on the subject ended, and since that time icons have been a major feature of Orthodox (Eastern) churches. Orthodox faith sees Jesus as the visible image of the invisible God, so that matter is sanctified as holy, and the human person is a fitting finite image of the unknowable divine being. Matter is, of course, only holy insofar as it expresses the divine. So it needs to be purified, freed from disordered desire, sanctified and united to God. The incarnation is the sanctification of matter. In Christ matter and spirit are inextricably united, so that the proper destiny of the whole material cosmos is to be united to the divine in Christ.

This is called 'theosis' by Orthodox theologians, the participation of the cosmos in the divine nature. Through the incarnation, God sanctifies matter by the divine presence. Through the cross, material nature turns away from itself and offers itself fully to God. And through the resurrection, material nature is taken into the divine life. All Christians may now enter this process, which is repeated or made present in the liturgy of the Church. They do so on behalf of the whole cosmos, and through them, as the meeting points of spirit and matter, the cosmos will be divinized. Icons are visual expressions of the meeting of finite and infinite, of matter and spirit, of time and eternity. As such, they mediate to Orthodox Christians the reality and the hope that they and all things will be interpenetrated, as Jesus was, by divine self-emptying love, so that they might grow by the power of the Spirit, and in the companionship of the Son, to share in the life of God.

The Orthodox path of spirituality was cultivated in a distinctively new form of religious life, the monastic community. Jesus' recorded advice to at least some disciples to renounce the world, to sell all possessions, to remain unmarried 'for the sake of the kingdom', and to be humble and childlike, has always been a puzzle for his followers. Is it meant to apply to all? And if so, how can the ordinary affairs of life be conducted? In grappling with this problem, the Church developed a distinction between obligations on everyone (like not killing or stealing) and counsels of perfection (based on Jesus' statement, 'If you wish to be perfect, go, sell your possessions, and give the money to the poor . . . then come, follow me': only in Matthew 19.21). The counsels apply only to those who have a special vocation to a life of poverty, chastity and obedience, who renounce the affairs of the world to devote themselves to prayer.

Jesus himself was apparently unmarried, had no property or home of his own, was wholly obedient to the Father's will, did not attempt to take any political role in Judaea, and allowed himself to be unjustly killed rather than attempt forceful defence. Those who seek to follow Jesus in an especially close way may thus wholly renounce the desire for wealth, sex and power, withdrawing from the world into a community of those who seek to contemplate and find companionship with God alone.

Such a witness is necessarily for a minority. Christians have always held that wealth, sexuality and political power are in themselves good, and necessary for the good ordering of the world that God has created. It is good to gain and possess wealth that may be used for the relief of others. It is good to enjoy the sexual expression of committed love, and to raise a family in which love can be found. It is good to be in a position to exercise wisdom in ruling a society with justice and compassion. Yet wealth, sex and power should not be sought for their own sake, regardless of the love they should express. Not all are called to have great wealth, to found a family, or to political rule. Many are called to express love in routine and everyday tasks, in helping others in inconspicuous ways, and in faithfully carrying out the jobs in which they find themselves. It is an important Christian insight that each person has their own vocation and calling, rooted in the gifts and capacities God has given them. In discerning that vocation, whether it is seemingly prominent and historically decisive or relatively anonymous and ordinary, each person will find their own happiness and fulfilment.

To follow Jesus in a more demanding way, to give up all except the adoration of God, is a special vocation for the few who have the capacity for it. It is a witness to the world that God is the final goal of all desiring, and that to seek to know and love God more fully is the most important task of every human being. The monastic vocation does not impugn the goodness and beauty of the created world, or the importance of the social virtues. The monk will see God in the beauty of nature and in the social relationships of communal life. But God alone, and

God as disclosed in Jesus Christ and made present in the Spirit, is the focus and centre of the monastic life of prayer and worship.

Each day monks meet between three and seven times to sing or recite the Divine Office, largely composed of selections of Psalms and biblical readings, in which they praise and thank God for the blessings of life, and pray for the good of the world and for particular individuals known to them. They celebrate the Eucharist, the Great Thanksgiving, in which Christ is made present in bread and wine and his passion and resurrection are commemorated. And they usually engage in agricultural, manual or scholarly work, and undertake hospitality and charitable work for the poor and sick. It is a simple and regular routine, and its point is to discipline the mind to think always of God, to rest in the knowledge of the presence of God, and to unite the human soul in love to Jesus Christ.

So the Eastern Orthodox Church, centred on Constantinople, elaborated its faith in a three-fold God who sanctified the material world by uniting a human body and soul to itself in Jesus Christ, and who, by the action of the Holy Spirit, raises that world to participate in the divine nature. The icons of the Orthodox Church symbolize the divinization of the material, and in its monastic life there is a distinctive vocation and witness both to the renunciation of egoistic desire that is necessary if matter is to be fitted for divinization, and to the passionate desire for God alone that unites the soul eternally to God. This is a spirituality that has stood the test of all the ambiguities of the Roman Empire and the disasters of repeated militant attacks by hostile forces, and that endures today in the 14 or 15 national self-governing churches of the Orthodox Communion.

33
The Eastern Church

The Church paid a price for becoming the official religion of the Roman Empire. It became entangled in the intrigues of the imperial court. Its senior clergy wore the robes of the aristocracy, and were often themselves aristocrats. The emperor appointed bishops, convened Church councils, and effectively took over much of the rule of the Church. The commemoration of the Last Supper, the central rite of the Church, began to imitate the formalized rituals of the court. The Church served the emperors' obsession with developing one unified system of belief throughout the empire, and forcefully repressing dissident, 'heretical' systems. It became complicit in the military defence of the Byzantine Empire as it began to crumble under external and internal attacks and rebellions.

Yet in all this, the Church continued to preach the gospel of the un-licensed preacher from Galilee who proclaimed a kingdom not of this world, and who was the friend of outcasts and the poor. Each day the Supper of the Lord was repeated. But now it became a drama, in which richly robed priests withdrew behind the iconostasis, the screen of icons behind which the sacred mystery of Christ's passion and resurrection was made present. Surrounded by candles, wreathed in incense, amidst the visual beauty of icons and mosaics and enclosed by the soul-piercing sounds of sacred music, the words of Jesus at the Last Supper in Jerusalem were repeated: 'This is my body'; 'This is my blood'. Here the risen Christ was truly present in the physical forms of bread and wine. Here the sacrifice of his life, offered so that the sins of the whole world should be for-given, completed once on the cross but offered always in eternity, was manifested again and again in each local place and time. Here his risen life was given to those who knelt in adoration before him, the food of eternity for the children of time.

Those who participated in this sacred drama could know and feel that God was present among them, that the divine life was surrendered for them so that they might be healed from despair and loss, and that Christ's life was given to them so that they could be raised in him to the life of God. Each church became a small image of the imperial court, graced by the presence of the emperor. But this was a court beyond all earthly courts, its emperor was the Prince of Peace, and to enter it was not only to enter a place of glory and beauty – it was to transcend time itself.

Few worshippers received the body and blood of Christ regularly in communion. For that, it came to be felt, confession of sins was required, so that one was fit to receive the life of the risen Lord. Instead, bread that had been blessed during the Great Thanksgiving, the Eucharist, was offered to all. It was enough to stand in the presence of the Holy Mysteries, where earth was taken into heaven, and to feel that here the deification of the earth and all its life was, however gradually and ambiguously, being effected.

As the early sharing of a simple meal deepened into a local presenta-tion of what St Athanasius described as the divine life becoming human so that earthly life could become divine, so remembrance of Jesus became the worship of the risen and glorified Christ, Lord and Judge of the universe. On the ceiling of most Orthodox churches, the face of Christ Pantocrator, Lord of All Things, looks down with compassion and kindness, but also with the severity of a just judge. As generations of worshippers reflected on the teaching of the early councils that Christ was truly God, and on the Eucharistic celebration of human par-ticipation in the life of God, so they came to have a greater sense of their companionship with the saints, those who were solely human and yet already transformed by the grace of God to share fully in the divine life.

At the Eucharist, worshippers felt themselves to be not only in the presence of God, but in the presence of angels and saints, of other forms of created being who stood in the presence of God, and of humans who had died and were close to God in wisdom and goodness. Among the saints, surely none was greater than Mary, mother of the Lord, who had nourished Jesus with her own blood in her womb, had known Jesus in his childhood and growing up, and had stood by the cross at his death.

The Council of Ephesus in AD 431 had given Mary the title of Theotokos, God-bearer, Mother of God. No one else on earth could stand in that position. No one else could have such an intimate relationship with the Son of God. If to be holy is to be filled with God, then her holiness was assured. She had assented to the angelic call to bear her divine Son, and she had been saluted by the angel as blessed above all women. So she has a unique place among the saints, among those who have died and who even now live more fully, as they share in the divine nature.

As Jesus was believed to be the divine Saviour, so Mary was thought of as the first of the redeemed, as a foreshadowing of the Church, bearing Christ within her own body and yet born in the Spirit of her own Son. Orthodox believers have always rejoiced in a sense of the 'communion of saints', the companionship of all Christians, living and dead. Reverence for Mary is a testimony to the belief that God is the God of the living, and not of the dead, and that the sanctified dead are alive with God. Reverence for the Mother of God is also a testimony to belief in Christ as fully divine, and not just a human being with a close relationship to the divine, as Mary undoubtedly was. She is revered as is anyone who is touched and graced by God. But she is the first of the redeemed, and the nearest of all to Christ the universal Saviour. If the saints in heaven can hold living persons on earth in their prayers, then Mary above all will pray to God for those who form the body of her Son, that they and all creation may come to know and love Christ in eternity as she undoubtedly did on earth.

The Orthodox Church looks very unlike the first fellowship of disciples in Jerusalem. It was a church that became allied with power and with earthly glory, and its destiny became to some extent intertwined with that of the Roman Empire of the East. But it was also a church that explored and deepened its faith in Jesus as the earthly embodiment of God by using all the resources of Greek philosophy and the best scientific knowledge of the day, and by developing sacred rituals of numinous beauty that were meant to express and foreshadow the raising of the whole temporal world to the realm of the eternal. Instead of a simple meal of fellowship, the Eucharist became an icon of the heavenly banquet of the saints, rejoicing in the presence of God and participating in the cosmic mystery of the Christ, the finite image of the invisible source and goal of all things. The daily liturgy of the Eastern Orthodox Church is not just the human remembrance of the life of one human being. It is a presentation and foreshadowing of the divine transfiguration of all created life into God, by the Spirit of Jesus, the one who gave his human life so that all might share the life of his divinity.

34
The Church and the Roman Empire

The Eastern Empire was to endure for just over a thousand years, but the Western Empire, centred on Rome, was prey to attacks by Vandals and other barbarians, and is usually said to have fallen in AD 476, when Odoacer, king of one of the Germanic tribes, deposed the last Western Emperor. Partly because of that, the bishopric of Rome was separated from imperial power, and the Patriarch of the West, the Pope, became a political power in his own right. As the old Western Empire fell, so the Latin Church grew, converting the Goths, Franks and other barbarian and militaristic tribal peoples to the Christian faith. In the continual power struggles of Western Europe, Charlemagne granted a large territory in Italy to the Pope, and was crowned Emperor by the Pope in AD 800. This attempted revival of a 'Holy Roman Empire' was never successful, and kept dividing, re-forming, and slowly shrinking, until it eventually disappeared from Europe in 1806.

The consequences for Christian faith were momentous. The political and spiritual claims of the papacy increased enormously, reaching their apogee with a declaration by Boniface VIII, in 1302, that all temporal power is subject to the Pope. This is rather a far cry from Jesus' statement that his kingdom was 'not of this world' (John 18.36), and it is not one that Roman Catholic theologians today would regard as either useful or correct. It shows a moment of complete assimilation of the political and religious realms, and it accounts for the strain of militarism that entered into medieval European Christianity, ambiguously allied with an empire under constant internal and external threat, and indeed doomed to collapse.

The Byzantine Empire too was doomed. Weakened by waves of attacks from barbarians and from the adjoining Persian Empire, and by revolts of its own subject peoples, it ceded most of the empire to the invading Arab armies of Islam in the seventh century. Already the imperial attempt to impose adherence to strictly defined doctrines had led to the breakaway of two great churches – the Church of the East and the six Oriental Orthodox Churches (including Egyptian Copts, Ethiopians and Syrians). Those churches today have about 30 million members in Middle Eastern countries, India and China. After the Arab invasion, in the ninth and tenth centuries, Serbia, Bulgaria and Russia became converts to Orthodoxy. But the last remnants of the Byzantine Empire were under repeated Muslim attack. In 1095 the Byzantines appealed to Pope Urban II for help against the invading Turks, and the result was the First Crusade. The Crusaders captured Jerusalem, but success was short-lived and the following crusades were largely catalogues of disaster. The Western Crusaders tried to erect a Latin kingdom in the Holy Land, and in the Fourth Crusade, in 1204, they sacked Constantinople, massacred its inhabitants, including the Orthodox Christians, and installed their own 'Latin' emperor. This reinforced the breach between Eastern and Western Christendom, and sealed the fate of the Byzantine Empire, which ceased to exist with the fall of Constantinople to the Turks in 1453.

Christian faith in its first millennium was entangled with the downfall of three empires. Its character was affected by that entanglement, as it wrestled with problems of power and military engagement. But it also had its effects, especially on the emerging nations of Europe and Russia. The Byzantine Church passed on its heritage of Greek science and philosophy to Islam, which achieved cultural pre-eminence in the ninth to the twelfth Christian centuries, and thereafter passed that heritage on to Western Europe. In Russia, which some called 'the third Rome', a great monastic tradition kept alive the call to holy poverty and contemplative prayer in a savage and turbulent land. The Roman Church reached out to tribal invaders and preached the gentle virtues of care for the old and sick, as well as the chivalric virtues of courtesy, loyalty and honour. Through centuries beset by warfare and pestilence, where human lives were often short and brutal, the Church offered God's forgiveness for sin and hope for the life of eternity. The crucifix, expressing God's identification with a world of pain and grief, became the central symbol of Catholic faith.

Augustine became the Catholic Church's definitive theologian. He introduced a note into Catholic theology that is lacking in the Orthodox tradition, that the whole human race is under penalty of death and hell because of the sin of Adam. This idea of 'original sin and guilt' is a sombre one, but is lightened by belief that Christ died on our behalf, so that we are redeemed from death and hell by the sacrifice of Christ, by the sheer grace of God and not by our good works or even our free acts of will.

The eleventh-century monk and Archbishop of Canterbury, Anselm, added that Christ offered to God the perfect obedience that we all owe to God, but cannot ourselves give. Since Christ's offering is of infinite value, however, we can use the merits of Christ's sacrifice to pay the reparation we owe to God for our continuing disobedience.

This rather legalistic idea of using the merits of Christ (and of the saints too) to satisfy God's justice played a very influential part in medieval Catholic religious life. In the doctrine of indulgences, which the Orthodox do not accept, the Pope claims the authority to use the Church's 'treasury of merit' to free people from the temporal punishments due to their sins. For a specific penitential act, the Church has power to reduce or even remit the temporal punishments of the dead in purgatory, the place of purification for those who are penitent, and who will attain the presence of God in heaven, but need first to be purified 'as if by fire', as the New Testament puts it (1 Corinthians 3.15).

In the medieval Catholic Church, the Eucharist, or Mass, is seen as a true sacrifice of propitiation to God, the merits of which can be applied to the living and to the penitent but as yet unperfected dead. The cross of Christ's sacrifice becomes the only means of human redemption from eternal death, and by its power alone the living and the dead are forgiven for their sins, and aided in their journey of self-purgation from death to eternal life.

The medieval Catholic view has a rather different focus from that of the Orthodox stress on the divinization of the cosmos as expressed in the incarnation and resurrection of the Christ. The Catholic emphasis on sin, on the cross, on sacrifice and the need for reparation, is darker. Yet everything in Catholic thought turns on the unmerited grace of God, the immensity of the sacrifice that liberates the human spirit from sin, and on our unending gratitude for a complete forgiveness that we do not have to earn.

Many of us may not resonate today with the idea that God condemns us before we act, or that God requires that divine honour should be satisfied, or that reparation and merit can be transferred from one person to another. There are other models and metaphors that we may prefer. But the proclamation of free and full forgiveness is still a gospel for the world, and Christ can still speak to us from the crucifix, as he did to St Francis, disclosing the broken heart of God in the midst of a suffering world.

35
Renaissance and Reformation

The Catholic Church was almost the only unifying and civilizing power in Western Europe after the collapse of the Western Roman Empire. Although itself involved in and compromised by the militaristic power struggles that rent Europe for centuries, it nevertheless, especially in its monasteries and cathedrals, kept alive traditions of classical scholarship, of charitable work and hospitality. Some medieval popes revelled in luxury and excess, but local clergy and monks were often devoted in prayer and active in pastoral care, and the Church's message of divine forgiveness and love was faithfully preached.

The grandeur of the great cathedrals, the beauty of Gregorian chant, the moral ideals of new orders like the Franciscans, and the intellectual excitement of the new church-founded universities balanced the savagery of competing nation states.

In the thirteenth century, Thomas Aquinas partly turned away from the Platonism that had influenced the early Church, and that had not been greatly interested in this world of appearances, to achieve a fusion of the newly rediscovered thought of Aristotle with Christian theology. This supported a more observational and experimental attitude to the natural world that was to encourage the rise of science. It enabled Christians to see revelation and grace as completely consistent with, yet completing, reason. And it laid the ground for a Christian humanism, which made human happiness and fulfilment a proper and natural aim that would be completed by the vision of God. From that time, Aquinas has been regarded as the most important theologian of the Catholic Church. Catholic theology has been committed in principle to the best available scientific view of the natural world, and to a humanistic morality based on investigation of human nature and its potentialities. But it has insisted that humans have a supernatural end in God, and thus that the natural world must properly be seen as intrinsically ordered towards the supernatural goal of happiness in God. The role of the Church is, through its sacraments, to mediate the grace of God that is needed to conform human lives to that supernatural goal.

From then until the sixteenth century art, music, literature and learning, largely through the patronage of the Church, blossomed. But at the same time, and partly for that very reason, discontent with the structures and practices of the Church grew. As scholars began to read the texts of the Bible more carefully, they questioned the luxury and hypocrisy of Church leaders. Often they desired to return to the simpler Christian life portrayed in the New Testament. In Prague, Jan Hus preached against corruptions in the Church, and called for all Christian beliefs to be tested by the New Testament alone. He was burned at the stake for heresy in 1415. But in 1517 Martin Luther posted 95 Theses against the corruption of the Church – particularly against the abuse of selling indulgences, which gave the impression that purchasers could buy their way out of purgatory – on the church door at Wittenberg, and the Protestant Reformation truly began.

Luther and most other 'Protestants', as they came to be called, like Calvin, wished to reform the Catholic Church, not leave it. But as attitudes hardened on both sides, a break became inevitable. Luther's drastic and decisive claim, accepted by all Protestants, was that salvation, acceptance by God, was 'by faith alone'. It was not a matter of accumulating merit by penances and good works, or by renouncing the world and living a highly disciplined life as a monk. It was not a matter of obtaining grace through church ceremonies, mediated and controlled by priests. It was not a matter of obedience to a church hierarchy, who reserved the sole right to interpret Scripture and define beliefs. It was a matter of pure grace, personally and directly given to all who placed their trust in Jesus Christ alone. The Bible, now for the first time available in print and in the vernacular, was open to all, who could read therein for themselves the simple gospel of Jesus. That gospel was of a kingdom of the heart, of the personal presence of the living Christ, of forgiveness not by priests and penances but by repentance and trust in the person of Jesus.

This turned out to be not so much a reform as a religious revolution. Jesus' preaching to the rural poor seemed to Protestants to contrast completely with the imperial papacy and aristocratic prince-bishops of the Catholic Church. The simple fellowship and shared meal of the Last Supper contrasted with the private offering by a solitary priest of the Mass in an archaic language as a propitiatory sacrifice for the souls of the dead. The ecstatic assemblies of the early Church, where people spoke in tongues and prophesied, contrasted with the highly ritualized ceremonies of a Solemn Mass with Gregorian chant, incense and candles in awe-inspiring basilicas modelled on the imperial assembly halls of Rome. Exclusive devotion to Jesus as Lord, the hope of resurrection with him, and his free forgiveness of sin, contrasted with widespread medieval devotion to Mary and the saints, doctrines of purgatory and indulgences, and the practice of private confession to a priest and church-imposed penances.

Here were two sets of religious dispositions and attitudes in sharp disagreement. Protestants wanted to preach a gospel of liberation from sin and personal fellowship with Jesus, so that people could hear the message clearly and respond to it by a conscious personal decision. They saw the Catholic Church of their day as offering a mechanical system of penance and merit by which people could buy their way into heaven without any free personal decision, and as replacing a fully personal relationship to Christ with external ceremonies and devotional cults to Mary and the saints that to some extent perpetuated worship of old pagan gods and detracted from the sole Lordship of Christ.

Misunderstandings abounded on both sides, but the root of the matter was a difference about the nature of Christian faith – whether it is a matter of the heart, of a personal and inner relation to God established by free decision, with no need of external trappings and ceremonies, or whether it is a matter of belonging to a visible, authoritative, divinely founded institution that uses every sensory means and external help to mediate divine grace to humans at many different stages of intellectual and spiritual understanding.

At the second Vatican council, in the 1960s, the Catholic Church officially embraced many Protestant requests – for Mass in the vernacular, widespread reading of the Bible, communion in both bread and wine, and freedom of conscience. Differences remain, especially about the teaching authority, the magisterium, of the Catholic Church, and about the interpretation of the Eucharist and the importance of the sacramental life of the Church. But on the whole it is now possible to see more clearly that these are two different approaches to Christian spirituality. The Roman Catholic view is that the visible unity of the Church and its properly authorized sacraments are of paramount importance. Protestant Christians think of the Church as the invisible communion of all those who put their trust in Jesus, and tend to regard personal relationship to Christ as more important than participation in external ceremonies. Perhaps these attitudes can now largely be seen as complementary approaches to the mystery of Christ, which can embrace both and forgive the more intemperate attitudes of each.

36
The Bible in a critical age

The sixteenth-century Protestant Reformation set in train a process that led inexorably to what is generally known as the European Enlightenment. For it established a right of dissent from religious and political authorities (the Roman Catholic Church and the Holy Roman Empire). It established the freedom to create new forms of religious belief and practice. It emphasized the right of individuals to interpret the Bible for themselves. It undermined habits of deference to tradition and belief in divinely established hierarchies. If liberty, equality and fraternity were to become the watchwords of political revolution in France in 1789, they were already leading ideas of the Protestant Reformers in the sixteenth century.

The classical Protestants, of course, wanted liberty to be under the sole authority of the Bible. But it soon became clear that many diverse interpretations of the Bible are possible, so that Protestant churches are continually splitting and dividing. Moreover, once the principles of criticism and personal interpretation were accepted, it was inevitable that the text of the Bible itself would come under critical scrutiny. With the publication of David Friedrich Strauss's *Life of Jesus* in 1835, it was clear that the Bible would henceforth be studied using all the methods of critical history. The biblical texts would be closely compared, their very diverse perspectives and the discrepancies between them would be noted, and attempts would be made to locate them in their probable historical contexts. The likelihood of their accuracy in recording historical events was assessed in the light of newly growing knowledge of scientific laws and more accurate investigations of alleged miracles. Greater awareness of the tendency to imaginative exaggeration and the literalization of dreams and visions in religion and in ancient histories generally led to a more sceptical approach to these ancient records. Archaeological investigations were to throw doubt on biblical records such as that of the invasion of Canaan by the Israelites. And as scientific knowledge of the evolutionary nature of the cosmos and of life on earth grew, so the literal accuracy of the book of Genesis was discredited.

The effect was sometimes wholly negative, a rejection of the divine inspiration of Scripture, of the truth of its historical claims about Jesus, and even of the existence of God. But there is another possibility. That is that the Bible cannot any longer be regarded as an inerrant literal record of historical events. It is better seen as a set of diverse and developing human interpretations of encounters with God, forming a cumulative tradition of response to a transcendent reality of supreme power and value. The Bible is 'inspired' by God in that the thoughts and experiences on which it is based, and the writing of its very varied texts and their editing and selection, were guided by God. Such guidance is not dictation, and it does not simply override human reasoning. It is more like a constant and cumulative influence on human minds by God as they discern the divine in thought and feeling. But such thoughts and feelings are culturally and psychologically formed, and what may be truly perceived is always fallibly interpreted and described. There can be inspired insight and authentic relation to the divine even though it is not inerrant, and even though it never wholly escapes the limitations of all human thought and experience.

The process is described in the earlier sections, 'The Hebrew Bible' and 'Jesus in the Gospels'. The prophets, Psalm-writers and storytellers of that collection of books can be thought of as people whose closeness to God raised their minds to new insights into divine wisdom, and enabled them to mediate divine power for healing or leadership. They were men and women filled with the Spirit of God – not a Spirit that made them infallible or dictated words to them, but a Spirit that enabled them to mediate, imperfectly but incisively, the divine reality to the human world. In the case of Jesus, too, the Gospels are not straightforward reportage of events, but reflections on the meaning of remembered or frankly reconstructed events in which the nature and purpose of God seemed to be disclosed in a new and revelatory way.

Many religions traditionally believe that their holy texts in some sense exist eternally, and are simply 'heard' by seers or prophets, and are divine in nature. The varied content and forms and literary styles of the Bible are not naturally conducive to such a belief. Once you have set aside belief that the Old Testament is inerrant, you are able to see it as a developing set of responses to perceptions of the divine within the Jewish community. The Hebrew prophets apprehended the divine as they encountered it in specific historical events, in which they discerned a providential purpose for their own historical destiny. And they apprehended the divine as a morally commanding presence that demanded their loyalty and a commitment to realize the divine purpose of establishing a society of justice and peace on the earth. These apprehensions were codified in the prophetic oracles and in the statutes and ordinances of the Law (Torah). Throughout the Hebrew Bible, a development of thought can be seen that moves to seeing these apprehensions as encounters with one creator of all things who has a moral purpose and vocation for all human beings. The Bible is the inspired record of that development, as a succession of prophets, poets and law-givers are prompted and guided by the Spirit to contribute to one cumulative tradition of response to the disclosures of God that have occurred in their history.

For Christians, the New Testament continues this process of development and rethinking as it finds in the remembered person of Jesus a focus and starting point for its distinctive perspective on the divine. Jesus is for Christians the paradigm event of encounter, in which new aspects of the divine nature and purpose are discerned. In Jesus, the divine command becomes a call to unlimited love, and the divine purpose is seen as the ultimate unity of the whole cosmos in Christ, the universal Wisdom of God. The whole Bible is then read by Christians in the light of that discernment. The New Testament documents record the earliest historical form of the revelation of God in Jesus, and thus have a peculiar and irreplaceable importance for Christians. But they do not preclude the possibility of new discernment, for through the Spirit Jesus remains a living presence in the Church, and many new possibilities of disclosure remain, with the one condition that they remain in conformity with the original pattern of the Gospel records of Jesus' life and teachings.

The Bible, in both Old and New Testaments, contains piercing insights, but it also contains lamentable blind spots. The key words are development and diversity. Beliefs about God and about the right human way of relating to God continually develop as general knowledge of the world is extended, and this development does not stop with either the Old or the New Testaments. They remain crucial documents for reminding us of the origins of our faith, but they point to the need for further progress. In such further development, diversity is unavoidable, as different approaches appeal to different people. All are freed from the illusory need to conform to one set of allegedly changeless beliefs. And all are required to tolerate and respect the conscientious interpretations of others, on the one condition that such interpretations do not cause obvious and avoidable harm.

Christianity can and should be a truly critical faith. Christians should be open to the most searching criticisms, and they must use all the tools of critical history in studying the Bible. But the Bible is in the end not a history book. It is a book of the prophetic discernments of the historical disclosures of God in the history of the Jewish people. To that ancient people modern Christians owe their own distinctive insights into the nature and purpose of God. We cannot be bound by ancient records. But we can see there the beginnings of our own understanding of God, and Christians find in the records of Jesus' life the definitive originating pattern of an authentic understanding of God. In that life Christians find prophetic discernment and historical disclosure united in one culminating moment of the tradition. Jesus, for Christians, is the one who supremely discerns the will and purpose of God, and in whom God discloses that will and purpose to the world. The New Testament is the earliest and definitive witness to that paradigm disclosure of God.

So the Bible should be read in such a way that the discernments it records can evoke corresponding but unpredictable and new discernments in us. In that way the Bible can be received as an inspired text, without any surrender of the critical principles that have transformed (or should have transformed) Christian understanding in the last two hundred years.

37
The new perspective of science

The rise of critical thinking in sixteenth-century Europe helped to inspire the greatest change in human consciousness since the discovery of methods of agriculture. This change was encapsulated in the conflict between Galileo and the Roman Catholic Church. In the thirteenth century the Church rediscovered the work of Aristotle, and a properly scientific approach to the natural world began. Unfortunately, Aristotelian science, with its commitment to changeless essences and ubiquitous final causality, turned out not to be a fruitful path for further understanding. The 'new science' which set aside such considerations and insisted on close observation and experiment, on rigorous measurement and the formulation of quasi-deterministic laws, was represented by Galileo and his telescope.

Galileo was silenced by the Inquisition, but he won the argument. The Aristotelian universe of intelligible essences and purposes gradually gave way to what became the Newtonian universe of observable physical properties and universal mechanistic laws. With Charles Darwin's *Origin of Species* in 1859, the principles of cumulative change from one physical kind of thing to another and the existence of a seamless continuum between them became part of the new scientific worldview.

In the twentieth century the rise of quantum physics placed some very large question-marks against the picture some had formed of a purely mechanistic, deterministic and predictable universe. It appears that the universe is more holistically interconnected, probabilistic and supramaterial than had been suspected. It is more like a multi-dimensional set of states in a mathematically constructed space than like a three-dimensional array of solid particles. This universe we see and in which we live is not the universe as it really is. There are, quantum physics suggests, vast and veiled realities beyond ours.

Physics seems again to be on the verge of radically new understandings of the universe. But certainly the cosmos is like nothing envisaged anywhere on earth before the sixteenth century. Earth is a small planet of a small star in a small galaxy in one universe among many other universes that may exist. Events occur in accordance with general, mathematically elegant laws that generate through a process of cosmic evolution a continuous series of emergent entities, including human beings. In the long run, according to the second law of thermodynamics, it seems likely that this cosmos will cease to exist, as it loses heat and energy, and all the complex and conscious forms to which it has given birth throughout its history perish. Long before that time, the human species is likely to have evolved, if it is lucky, into something very different and currently unimaginable.

If the Christian faith is to be understood in the context of modern science, old pictures of earth as the centre of creation and of humans as the goal of creation and the main denizens of heaven will have to be revised. If Christians say that 'Jesus is seated at the right hand of God', they cannot think that a young male human being sits uniquely close to the creator of what may be unlimited numbers of universes.

Fortunately the imaginative revision that is required is not as drastic as it may seem. Christ is the eternal Word and Wisdom of God, far beyond any finite form, but containing all finite forms, the archetypes of endless worlds. The human archetype is only one of these possibilities in the mind of God, and Christ transcends them all, while being capable of self-manifestation in many. In this universe, in this galaxy, on this planet,

Christ is manifested in human form. The human person of Jesus is able truly to embody the eternal Christ, though he is only one embodiment of the infinite divine Word. Jesus, the human incarnation of God, takes humanity into the divine being. The Word descends to become incarnate, and because of that unity of divine and human, humanity itself ascends to become divine, to participate in the divine nature, as this form of evolved, material, embodied personhood is taken into the reality of God.

Humans have evolved from other forms of organic life, and they may evolve again beyond humanity. But humanity has been touched and transformed by the divine, and for that reason human beings will always be able to grow in the knowledge and love of God, and they will always be capable of mediating the power and wisdom of God in their particular finite form. Jesus the Christ will always be their King, the definitive image of God for them and the mediator of God's fulfilling power for their lives.

In a wider life beyond this earth and beyond this universe, they may come to know other forms of Christ, and rejoice that the infinite Wisdom of God can truly be known in their own form, though it surpasses every finite form. This is not really a new doctrine for Christian faith. It was believed by those who framed the orthodox creeds, though they had little knowledge of the vast extent of the cosmos. It requires only an extension of imagination, so that heaven is not seen as a purely human preserve. It is where countless forms of God may be expressions that truly mediate the divine life and yet point beyond themselves to the true and humanly incomprehensible infinity of the divine being.

These things we cannot know now. But the imagining of them shows the power of new scientific knowledge to extend and enrich appreciation of the glory, power and wisdom of the creator, who, on the Christian view, identifies with all creation to transfigure and take it into the divine life. The Christian hope, based on the apostolic testimony to the resurrection and ascension of Jesus, is that our present human lives will be transfigured and taken into God. Humans may not be the centre of creation. But these temporal lives can be raised by God to the life of eternity, as the life of Jesus was. The Christian hope is for the apotheosis of time itself, a process in which humanity can play a small but significant part.

38
Critiques of traditional morality

Two important facets of the European Enlightenment were the acceptance of methods of informed critical enquiry in regard to history and religion, and the development of the modern scientific worldview. These had an impact on the Christian use of historical material in the Bible, and on the Christian view of the universe as God's creation. But they also had an impact on the Christian view of morality.

If we take a critical view of the Bible, we are not likely to believe that particular ethical recommendations in the Bible are binding for all people at all times. We are more likely to say that such recommendations represent the deliberations of minds inspired by disclosures of God, but nevertheless imbued to some degree with the cultural and psychological limitations of their time.

This is very obvious with some of the ethical rules of the Old Testament, like the command to exterminate all the Amalekites (Deuteronomy 25.19), or to stone disobedient children to death (Deuteronomy 21.18–21). But what goes for the Old Testament also goes for the New. The Gospels record that the apostles frequently misunderstood Jesus – James and John, for example, wished to call down fire on towns that had rejected Jesus (Luke 9.54), and none of them could make out what Jesus meant by 'rising from the dead'. These misunderstandings are unlikely to have stopped after Pentecost. When Paul writes that women should keep silent in church, or obey their husbands, or that slaves should obey their masters, he has not seen the moral challenge of the unlimited love that Jesus taught and practised.

We must rethink many New Testament moral teachings. Few would really think that we should never swear on oath or call anyone 'Father', even though both prohibitions are apparently uttered by Jesus in Matthew's 'Sermon on the Mount'. (Matthew 5.34; 23.9). Few, I hope, would think that Jesus will come in flaming fire to wreak vengeance on those who do not obey the gospel (2 Thessalonians 1.7–8). The fact is that the moral insights of the New Testament writers, even though inspired to new heights by Jesus, had not matured to the point where they could see what unlimited divine love requires and allows. Christians must continue to rethink these teachings, in the light of the disclosure of God's love in Jesus.

Paul was himself fairly clear about this: 'The letter kills, but the Spirit gives life', he wrote (2 Corinthians 3.6). All the commandments of Torah are summed up in the rule to love your neighbour as yourself: 'Christ is the end of the Law' (Galatians 5.14). It would be supremely ironic if Christians took the moral recommendations of the man who wrote these words as a new law or written code. Christians must live by the Spirit, and the Spirit may have new things to teach about what love requires. We should look carefully at the recommendations of the New Testament writers – after all, they were closer to Jesus than we are. On the other hand, we have had two thousand years to reflect on these teachings in very different contexts. And so we should not hesitate to reject recommendations where (but only where) they seem to fall short of the standard of the forgiving, reconciling love that we see disclosed in Jesus.

Moral principles must be worked out with patience and sensitivity, paying regard to all the complexities of different circumstances. Specific rules, whether found in the Bible or in pronouncements of Christian churches, usually express cultural limitations as well as insights, and so they can rarely be regarded as absolute. A study of history shows that such pronouncements have often varied, and have sometimes been mistaken. We may want to take them as the considered advice of scholarly, prayerful and informed Christian leaders. But we may also remember the Reformation principle that even pious Christian leaders may err, and reserve the right to form a conscientious moral decision of our own, where we can adduce strong reasons for that.

Perhaps the only truly absolute biblical rules are the two Jesus picked out (Matthew 22.36–40) – love God (which entails respecting what God has created, and seeking to do what God wills for creation) and love your neighbour as yourself (where your neighbour is anyone in need, as the parable of the Good Samaritan makes clear).

There is a proper area of moral autonomy, of responsible human decision-making, in all complex human situations. But human free choice is not the last word for a Christian. Christian choices must be directed to the final good of union with God, and participation in the wisdom and love of God. That transcendental reference gives Christian morality a special depth and intensity. Christian morality is not a morality of unquestioning obedience to sheer unexplained commands. It is a way of love for and delight in God, whose goodness alone is absolute, and whose will for the world is that it should progress towards sharing in and being transfigured by divine goodness. Christians should do what is right because of their love for God, who is supreme beauty and perfection. Their love is to be taken into and transfigured by God's own love for creation. Participation in that dynamic and creative love, not strict obedience to written rules, is the most adequate basis for a biblically informed Christian morality.

39
Morality and purpose

Mainstream Christian moral teaching has not in fact been based on the direct application of biblical rules to very diverse human situations. In the Catholic tradition it has been, and still is, based on 'natural law', which is basically an Aristotelian and Stoic conception, baptized into Christianity. This law is natural in four ways – it does not depend on revelation; it is knowable by reason; it takes its principles from a study of human nature; and it seeks to discern and safeguard the purposes of nature. In its Christian form, it appeals to the fact that God has created the cosmos and human nature for a purpose. This purpose is that natural objects should realize the potentialities that God has implanted in them. Human beings have a special place in creation, for they are made in the image of God – with the capacity for understanding, responsible creativity, co-operation, compassion and affection. Humans, too, should realize their God-given potentialities, and we can discover what these are by analysis of the natural inclinations and desires of human beings. For 'good' is, as Aristotle said, the natural object of a reasonable (not self-defeating or harmful) desire.

For example, sexual desire and activity has the purpose of procreation; and the natural inclinations to happiness and sociability are symptoms of purposes to achieve natural goods created by God. Morality enjoins that we should not frustrate these purposes of nature, but we may pursue them as natural goods in accordance with the maxims of prudence (they must not directly cause harm to ourselves or others) and justice (all persons must be taken into consideration).

The basis of this morality is the doctrine of creation, with the implication that God has ordered the natural world for a good purpose. Jesus (and, for Catholics, the magisterium of the Church) adds to this natural morality our ordering to the supernatural end of friendship with God, and knowledge of that supernatural end helps to ensure that our desires will be shaped to lead us towards that end, and not away from it. For the Catholic tradition, grace fulfils and completes nature, but nature is good and its basic purposes are those of God.

However, just as modern science challenged the Aristotelian world-view in general, so it throws doubt on the traditional idea that nature has purposes which should never be frustrated. (For Aristotle, all things have 'final causes' or goals that they naturally strive to realize.) Modern science sees nature as evolving consciousness as an emergent reality by processes of random mutation and natural selection. It is reasonable to see this process as planned by God in order that intellectual and morally responsible agents should come to exist. But it is not possible to hold that every part of this process is just as God directly wills it to be. God has a purpose – that nature should evolve persons – but the purpose is achieved by a probabilistic or partly random process. The process has a purpose, but many specific parts of it are blind alleys, dead ends, or even deleterious to the general purpose. For instance, the flourishing of cancer cells is part of the process of emergent evolution, and the nature of evolution entails that cancer may come to exist as an entirely natural phenomenon. But cancer is not a 'purpose of nature', and it often frustrates the general purpose of the flourishing of persons.

For such an evolutionary view, the purpose of nature is to develop personal forms of life. Physical and biological processes should be frustrated wherever they impede such a purpose, and they should be improved wherever possible to expedite it. The flourishing of persons comes first, and biological processes must be subordinate to that end. Sexual activity is not just for the purpose of procreation. When sex exists in a fully personal realm, it expresses loyal and faithful love, and that purpose may often be more important than the purely biological one. It may even conflict with purely biological processes, and in such cases it may no longer be considered an absolute rule that we should not frustrate any alleged purpose of nature. The biological 'purpose' needs to be subordinated to moral considerations of the flourishing of persons.

A good Christian basis for morality is that the world is God's creation, and that therefore the world has a positive and good purpose. But in the modern scientific context, that purpose is best seen as the flourishing of personal life, and that may involve 'interfering with' natural processes in a responsible way to remove pain and disadvantage, and to increase the possibilities for fuller personhood.

Among the crucial moral issues for our age are conservation of the planet's resources and proper respect for the earth as God's good creation; removal of the gross injustice whereby the majority of the earth's population starve while people in the developed world live in luxury; removal of all disadvantaging forms of sexual or ethnic discrimination; and promotion of non-violence and greater respect for all sentient life on earth. The consideration that God creates the world to be enjoyed in due measure by all sentient beings, and gives to humans the responsibility for 'tilling and keeping' the earth (Genesis 2.15), should make these issues priorities for all Christians. God's purpose is that we should make the earth a place where beauty and friendship flourish, and where all creatures can share in that flourishing. The incarnation of Christ on earth makes nature itself holy; as Christians are the body of Christ on earth, we are called to be the priests, guardians, healers and lovers of the earth. That is the unavoidable obligation of all Christians, for 'faith by itself, if it has no works, is dead' (James 2.17).

40
German liberal Christianity

From the sixteenth century on in Europe the application of the methods of critical thought and history to the Bible, the growth of a new scientific worldview, and the realization of new moral possibilities like participatory democracy, capitalism, an extension of the range of human choice, and technological innovation in medical and sexual matters, had a marked effect on forms of Christian faith. This is most clearly expressed in various forms of German liberal Protestantism in the nineteenth and twentieth centuries.

The German theologian Friedrich Schleiermacher (1768–1834) is sometimes called 'the father of liberal theology'. Accepting that Christian faith could not be demonstrated by rational argument or appeal to biblical evidence, he proposed that the most important foundation of faith is personal experience. This he calls 'feeling', the subjective pole of an apprehension of the 'infinite and eternal' in and through the things of finitude and time. Religion, he writes, in his *Speeches on Religion*, is 'a sense and taste for the Infinite', or as he puts it in a later work, translated into English as *The Christian Faith*, the basic religious intuition is 'a sense of absolute dependence' upon one 'Supreme and Infinite Being', the total dependence of one's being on a reality that is absolutely independent and self-existent.

This is a special sort of intuition or form of consciousness, a sense of something interfused with and known through events and places in time and space, but remaining unbounded by them, as a transcendent, unique and indefinable presence. Schleiermacher calls it 'God-consciousness', and it is the basis and heart of any living religious faith.

To be fully conscious of God is no merely theoretical or passive awareness. It is to become one with what one truly knows, to be filled with the presence of God, as an active and transforming power. It is to realize a personal union of finite human nature and the infinite divine essence, and to become a mediating channel of the eternal in the midst of time: 'To be one with the infinite in the midst of the finite and to be eternal in a moment, that is the immortality of religion' (*Second Speech on Religion*).

Most human beings are not truly conscious of God, but are in bondage to egoism and greed, to a false independence that shuts out awareness of the total dependence of the self on the eternal. Jesus was uniquely God-conscious, and in him egoism was destroyed; his God-consciousness was the 'veritable existence of God in Him' (*The Christian Faith*, § 94).

The mediating power of that divine–human unity generated the Church, a new form of corporate life, in which the Spirit continues to unite human lives and the divine essence in a fellowship in which 'everything is related to the redemption accomplished by Jesus of Nazareth' (§ 11). In that community, persons are moved from alienation to unity – that is, redemption – and this is an act not of their own, but an act accomplished in them by the Spirit released into the world by Jesus' perfect God-consciousness.

For Schleiermacher Christian faith is not intellectual acceptance of dogmas. It is a transforming personal experience of God, an apprehension of the eternal in time that unites the finite and the infinite. Nothing is required for Christian faith that does not directly underlie such apprehension. So, he writes, a visible resurrection, ascension or return of Jesus, or the literal performance of his miracles, are not essential to faith. With regard to such things, he says, 'All that can be required of any Protestant Christian is that he shall believe them insofar as they seem to him to be adequately attested' (§ 99).

This is a form of faith that can live easily with radical biblical criticism, new scientific knowledge and changing moral insights. Later German liberals like Albrecht Ritschl (1822–1889) and Adolf Harnack (1851–1930) stressed morality more and experience less than Schleiermacher. But they too tended to reject metaphysical dogmas as 'Hellenistic' intrusions into early Christianity, and saw the Church primarily as a community committed to realizing Jesus' moral ideal of the 'kingdom of God', the fellowship of those whose hearts are inwardly ruled by God. Christianity is an inner ethical monotheism, whose vocation is to promote 'the rule of the holy God in the hearts of individuals' (Harnack, *What is Christianity?*, lecture 8).

German liberal theology was a little hard on Hellenistic metaphysics – the Gospels stress the role of the person of Jesus as more than a moral teacher, and Christianity does have intellectual beliefs that perhaps need to be correlated more positively with those of the sciences. But the liberal emphasis on personal experience of God and on an inwardly transforming moral commitment arising from that experience is a positive and permanent contribution to Christian understanding. It is not enough to ascertain historical facts about Jesus, to assent to the orthodox creeds, or to have a well-developed philosophical worldview. Christian faith is primarily rooted in transforming experience of an infinite and eternal supreme reality, mediated in and through Jesus of Nazareth and the churches that exist in his name. It is the inward rule of the Spirit of God in human hearts, the mediation of eternity in the midst of time.

41
The twentieth century

In the twentieth century many theologians have felt that the German liberal position is inherently unstable. It seems to lack a firm basis in the Lordship of Christ, who might be little more than the historical originator of the purely experiential and ethical fellowship of the Church.

In opposition to this tendency, the Swiss theologian Karl Barth (1886–1968) reasserted the centrality of the doctrines of the incarnation and the Trinity, and the primacy of the Bible not as a set of human documents, but as a unitary revelation whose author is God.

Barth accepted critical study of the Bible, but held that nevertheless the Bible should be read as a narrative that God uses to challenge all human worldviews and to witness to Jesus, the divine Word incarnate. Jesus was not a moral teacher subsumed under a Hellenistic myth, and the Bible is not just a collection of religious essays and letters. Jesus is the divine Wisdom embodied as fully as it can be in a human life for the sake of redemption, the uniting of estranged humanity to God, and the Bible is a divinely inspired set of human responses to the divine self-revealing activity that led up to and extends on from that unique divine incarnation.

In fact the classical liberal position often presupposed such views. For example, Harnack wrote that in Jesus 'the divine appeared in as pure a form as it can appear on earth' (*What is Christianity?*, lecture 8), and Schleiermacher believed that Jesus was uniquely sinless and God-conscious. Such beliefs do seem to need greater doctrinal support than the classical liberals overtly provided. Paul Tillich (1886–1965) and John Macquarrie (1919–) attempt in different ways to provide such support. Christian faith offers answers to existential questions necessarily involved in human existence – questions of guilt, finitude, the threat of meaninglessness and of moral ambiguity. It offers the power of New Being to live an authentically human life with courage and hope. That New Being is rooted in the power of Being-itself, which is a unique source of all beings without itself existing as an individual being, a 'being among others'. Being-itself is expressed in the world of finite objects – our world – which because of its separate and distinct existence is to some extent estranged or alienated from God, the source of its being. But the Spirit works within all things to reunite all sentient creatures into a commonwealth of love.

In Jesus the raising of human nature to its highest level enables holy Being, which is the power of love, of letting-be, to manifest itself. The incarnation is historically unique, and yet it is a natural human possibility that divine and human should be made one. And it is a possibility not just for a few, but for all, even though in a fallen world its normative expression in Jesus must be by pure divine initiative.

There are unexpected echoes of the thirteenth-century theologian Thomas Aquinas here. For he wrote of God as 'Being-itself' (*actus purus*, pure act), and saw divine grace as perfecting, not contradicting, nature and the deepest spiritual aspirations of all humanity. So it is perhaps not surprising that the Catholic theologian Karl Rahner (1904–1984) should also have developed a rich doctrinal view of God's self-giving and uni-tive activity in all creation, with Jesus not as its only instance, but as the clear and decisive declaration in human history of God's universal self-communication in love.

Emphasis on God's universal love for the world, on Jesus as its paradigm case, and on the Church as the instrument of divine love leads naturally to a much greater stress on possibilities of social and economic liberation. Love seeks to liberate the objects of its affection from harm, and from all that constrains opportunities for their proper flourishing and well-being. The Church has learned to its cost that too great an association with political power is corrupting. Yet it seems insufficient to preach a wholly spiritual freedom and fulfilment when millions are dying of starvation or live in conditions of deprivation or oppression.

The latter half of the twentieth century saw the rise of theologies of liberation, like those of Jürgen Moltmann (1926–) and Gustavo Gutiérrez (1928–). Such theologies recover the Old Testament sense of the importance of societies in which persons can flourish. 'Salvation' in the Old Testament was primarily the liberation of the people of God from their enemies. 'The kingdom of God' whose drawing near was proclaimed by Jesus is a society, and the vocation of the Church is to seek to make that society real. The Church cannot do so by pre-scriptive power or by the use of violence. But it may do so by serving the world in love, and by helping to remove barriers of class, race and sex that diminish some human lives relative to others.

In our grossly unequal world, the Church must adopt an 'option for the poor', to be on the side of the dispossessed, to dispel prejudice and indifference. As Jesus was in his own person a sacrament of the divine will, so the Church as the body of Christ should seek to make the world in which humans live transparent to the divine presence and purpose. The role of the Church in the world is not to provide a secure path to heaven for a few who will escape the general doom of the world. It is to work, through acts of charity and reconciliation, for the liberation of every human being, and even, so far as it is possible, for the liberation of all created things, from all that frustrates the fulfilment of their God-created capacities.

The positive achievements of the Enlightenment are irreversible. Accepting informed critical enquiry, Christian faith can be firmly founded on a transformative personal experience of God in Christ. Accepting the worldview of science, however provisional it is, Christian faith can be firmly placed in the context of a divinely ordained cosmic evolution. Accepting a moral emphasis on personal welfare, Christian faith can be firmly committed to enhancing the flourishing, so far as is possible, of all sentient beings, and especially of the disadvantaged. Such a Christian faith is well prepared to play a positive and creative role in the post-Enlightenment world of the twenty-first century.

42
Global Christianity

Christianity is a West Asian religion, and it has existed as a minority faith throughout Asia from its beginnings. But it was in Europe that it flourished most spectacularly, and from Europe it expanded in three main waves to become the world's largest religion. In the sixteenth century Spain and Portugal established Catholic empires in South America. In the seventeenth and eighteenth centuries, the French and British colonized North America, and in the late nineteenth century, their empires extended to Africa, Australia and the South Pacific.

In the twenty-first century Christianity has declined markedly in influence within Europe, but it is strong in the Americas, and growing in Africa and Asia. In 1992 there were estimated to be almost two billion Christians, about a third of the world's population, living in virtually every country in the world. Of course there are many different types of Christianity – not just Catholic, Protestant and Orthodox – and Pentecostals, largely independent churches stressing the gift of 'speaking in tongues', are the fastest-growing group.

The post-Enlightenment faith represented in this book is probably held by a minority of Christians in the world. Numerically, Christianity as a world faith is strongest in the global South, and it is hard to tell how it will develop. The influence of missionaries from North America and Europe established a theological standpoint that sometimes distances itself from liberalism, though in my view this is due to an unjustified fear of critical and scientific thought that will in time die away. The concerns of faith in the developing world lie elsewhere.

There is a concern to distance Christian faith from its colonial and imperial legacy, and find more indigenous cultural forms for its expression. So there are positive attempts to adapt Latin American, African or East Asian thought-forms and practices, just as Greek and Latin cultures shaped European Christianity. This means a celebration of the diversity of human cultures, and a dissolution of the idea that Christianity must take the same form everywhere. The Spirit will always promote friendship, reconciliation and respect for others. But the Spirit may take many forms, and perhaps the chief lesson of global Christianity is that the only adequate model of the Church today is acceptance of a diversity of perspectives held within a shared allegiance to the God who is disclosed and understood in various ways in and through Jesus. This model was expressed by the founding of the World Council of Churches in 1948.

The first World Parliament of Religions in 1893 pointed to an even wider cultivation of friendship between diverse world faiths. An attempt at greater mutual understanding between different religious traditions, without attempting to enforce agreement, would be an important factor in decreasing hostility and suspicion between the different cultures of the world. Christianity is bound to the principle of love of enemies (Matthew 5.44). While the word 'enemies' includes those who seek to do harm, it also includes intellectual opponents, those from whom one differs on basic matters of belief. Love entails making an attempt to understand and respect, so far as possible, those who differ in this way. So Christians have a duty to encourage inter-faith conversation, and this is especially important in areas where ethnic and religious markers of identity coincide and increase the dangers of social violence.

A second major concern of Christianity in the developing world is the concern with international social and economic injustice. There are no easy answers to such complex problems, but one basic Christian principle is clear – that priority should be given to the poor and oppressed, since Christ came to fill the hungry with good things and to send the rich away empty (Luke 1.53). The voices of the Christian South are rightly raised against the new colonialists of West and East who seek economic dominance and privilege, and in favour of those – women, child labourers and migrant workers – who cannot speak for themselves. Here, in our world, the ancient Christian virtues of care for the sick and elderly, for the young and illiterate, for political prisoners and refugees, are called for on a scale never before envisaged.

In many ways – in the Red Cross and other organizations for emergency aid, in the South African Truth and Reconciliation Commission, in the Jubilee 2000 campaign for remitting the unpayable debts of the poorest countries, and in thousands of individual efforts to build bridges of common humanity – Christianity continues to witness in action to God's love for the world for which Christ gave his life. The often vibrant life and exuberant witness of non-Western Christians promises an exciting future for global Christianity as it escapes the long shadow of the Roman Empire and moves into the rainbow light of a many-cultured world. In that world its vocation is to bring reconciliation, friendship, light and the hope of resurrection life to all nations and peoples. 'You are the light of the world', said Jesus (Matthew 5.14). What light chiefly does is to reveal and clarify the distinctive and unique character of the objects it illuminates. That is the vocation of the Church in the world of today.

The final goal of creation

43
The future

Matthew relates that Jesus commanded the apostles to 'make disciples of all nations' (Matthew 28.19). In the twenty-first century every nation of the world has encountered Christianity in some form. But it looks fairly certain that Christianity will never become the faith of the whole world. There will always be those who cannot accept the Christian faith, who follow different spiritual paths, or who reject religious viewpoints altogether. In a global context Christianity needs to accept a humbler role as a community of the Spirit of Christ that invites others to join its fellowship, but that respects and seeks positively to love – to enjoy and help so far as is possible – all who remain outside. More like Judaism than it has been, Christianity would renounce all claim to be the one vehicle of human salvation. It would be a fellowship called by God to a vocation to witness to the God of limitless love disclosed in Jesus, to be guided by the Spirit in seeking to share in that divine love, and to live in peace and positive co-operation with its neighbouring faiths and world outlooks.

It is impossible to predict the future, and there are certainly many possibilities of opposition, hatred, misunderstanding and conflict in the world. But hope is a theological virtue, and the hopeful path is that Christianity may be able to be a peacemaking and reconciling force in the world. The document 'Towards a Global Ethic', drafted by Hans Küng for the 1993 Parliament of World Religions and signed by representatives of all world religions present, is an attempt to spell out some of the main issues involved in such reconciliation. Four key issues are noted: commitment to a culture of non-violence and respect for human life; to a just economic order; to tolerance and truthfulness; and to equal rights and partnership between men and women. That, it seems to me, is a strong basis for co-operation between religions, and since Christians say that Christ 'has given us the ministry of reconciliation' (2 Corinthians 5.18), Christians have a special part to play in such a process.

It is very unlikely that, in the foreseeable future, diversity of religious belief will disappear or be merged into some new form of world religion. It is more likely that many diverse forms of religious belief will flourish, and many of them will insist on their distinctness and difference from others. In all this diversity, however, it is also likely that there will be parts of most major religious traditions that, embracing new scientific knowledge and critical approaches to scripture and doctrine, are able to forge closer bonds of fellowship and unity. Insofar as a tradition is open to informed and principled revision, is concerned to see its place within the global pattern of religions, and accepts the partial nature of all human thought, old boundaries between religions may fade away. Differences of approach, in the use of key metaphors, in spiritual practice and in historical traditions, will remain, but a global ecumenism of religions may come to exist.

In such an ecumenism, diverse religions will not stand in hostile opposition to one another. There will be a continual exchange of insights, without any pressure to adopt one dominant system of doctrines. Christianity, for instance, could be seen not as the only, exclusive truth about the world, but as the Christian path to unity with the Supreme Wisdom and Goodness that is the ultimate source of all being. Global unity-in-diversity could become a major ideal for such strands of religion, and this is an ideal that those who are sympathetic to the form of Christian thought expressed in this book may well espouse, but would never seek to enforce. If humans have a very long future ahead of them, it is possible that such an ideal might be realized.

It is also possible, however, that humans, who have the capacity to destroy the world through nuclear and biological means, may bring all human life to an end fairly soon. Then there will be little historical future. Even if that does not happen – and Christians should pray that it does not – life on earth will become impossible in about five thousand million years, when the sun will die. If our species survives that event by going out into deep space, then most cosmologists currently think that the universe itself will eventually run out of energy, and end with a whimper, not a bang, as all the galaxies and stars burn out and leave only a long, dark, cold emptiness in which no energy or life can exist.

It is on the limits of possibility that we may learn before then how to re-embody ourselves in a different space-time, and continue to transfer, by methods scarcely conceived as yet, to new and younger universes for ever, in which case physical life will be literally unending. But 'we' would obviously be very different from members of the human species. Our successors might be vast intelligences or information systems, but they would not be 46-chromosomed primates with four limbs and a sensory nobble on top. It seems certain, then, that the human species will become extinct, however long it takes. Our species began, and it will end. If that takes hundreds or thousands of millions of years, will Christian faith then exist?

The Christian faith, as I see it, is that there is a creator who wills communities of intelligent persons to exist, whatever their physical form. There is an eternal Wisdom on which all finite forms are patterned, and in which they will be united. This Wisdom was embodied on earth in the human person of Jesus, and from his life sprang the many communities of the Church, inwardly guided by the Spirit who had filled and informed Jesus' life. God knows and remembers all that happens in all created worlds, and so all things are held inalienably in the divine mind. God wills that all created persons should find the fulfilment of the life they have chosen in that unbounded divine awareness. For humans, this means that they will be re-embodied in new worlds that God creates, where they can find an appropriate completion of their earthly lives. In those worlds they will see and know that the eternal Wisdom had in fact been embodied in their world, even if they had not perceived him, and that in and through his self-offered human life he had in fact opened the way from earth into the wider life of God, even if they had not realized it. All will then see Christ, the eternal Wisdom in human form, and their earthly lives will be assessed in the light of his infinite love and compassion.

If this is the heart of Christian faith, then it will exist as long as humans exist. We may suppose that it will exist long after humans have ceased to exist, for it will always remain true that God entered the estranged world of humanity in order to raise it to participation in the divine life. That redemption is for them and for their descendants, however remote and different in physical form. Indeed, it is for all the galaxies there ever have been or will be, though God's Wisdom may take other forms in other galaxies, and the eternal Christ may have a myriad forms and faces.

Whether the human future is short or long, it will come to an end. The conditions of human life may improve, though greed, hatred and ignorance are likely to remain as long as humans remain morally free. But Christian hope is not for continual improvement and unending life in this physical universe: 'If for this life only we have hoped in Christ, we are of all people most to be pitied' (1 Corinthians 15.19). Christian hope is for life in God, and that is not just for the final survivors in a physical race for perfection. It is for all who have died at any point in the temporal history of the cosmos, that they might all share in the life of eternity.

44
The resurrection of the dead

Christian faith is absolutely, unequivocally good news. Jesus said, 'The time is fulfilled, and the kingdom of God has come near; repent, and believe in the good news' (Mark 1.15) – the presence and power of God has come near to you; turn away from greed, hatred and egoism, and accept the Spirit of abundant life.

Christian faith is good news for everyone without exception: 'We have our hope set on the living God, who is the Saviour of all people'

(1 Timothy 4.10). There is no one who has ever lived or who will ever live on earth who is born without the possibility of salvation – salvation from greed and selfishness and the destruction and despair they bring, by participating in the life of God.

Like the Judaism from which it sprang, Christianity is not concerned solely with life after death. It is concerned with life more abundant on earth, with enjoyment of the good things of creation and with a passion that they should be shared as widely and fully as possible. Part of that enjoyment is conscious fellowship with God, known through the Spirit in the heart, patterned on the remembered life of Jesus of Nazareth, on his forgiving love, his death to self and resurrection to new life: 'You show me the path of life. In your presence there is fullness of joy; in your right hand are pleasures for evermore' (Psalm 16.11).

For many centuries ancient Jewish thought had little or no concern with life after death. But it was inevitable that thought should turn to those many people for whom God willed life, yet who seemed to have no experience of the joy of life or of the divine presence. Were their lives to end without any sense or feeling of the presence of God? Were they, as they continued to be remembered for ever by God, to be remembered only as frustrated and unfulfilled lives?

There were also those who suffered torture and death at the hands of their enemies, faithful to God yet living and dying in pain and anguish. And there were those who killed them, those who hated life itself and sought to destroy it in their lust for power and wealth, and yet who seemed to prosper. How could a just and merciful God, who knows and remembers all things, who cares for all creation, and who has the power to make all things new, rest content with such uncompleted lives?

So there arose, in some late Old Testament writings, the idea of the resurrection of the dead. For the Hebrew tradition, it was important that human persons are embodied. Bodies enable knowledge of a physical environment to be obtained through the senses. They enable persons to act in specific ways within such an environment. And they enable persons to encounter and co-operate with one another as socially related beings. Yet bodies change quite radically over the years, and human consciousness, feeling, memory and intention could in principle be embodied in other ways. So the idea of a 'new body' in which the same conscious personality could exist is an intelligible one.

In a resurrected body, persons could continue in a new environment to know and love God better, or could have a life in which they could be rewarded for their moral endeavours, or punished for their moral failures. The justice of God could be vindicated, and the will of God that all should share in the divine life could become a reality.

There were many different ways of thinking about resurrection, but it became for many Jews a hope for closer and deeper awareness of God than had been possible during earthly life. When Jesus appeared to the disciples after his death, resurrection took on a new and more forceful meaning. Those appearances were of a body that existed in a different form of reality beyond this space and time (though it could manifest itself physically here). Hope for resurrection became central to Christian faith, as hope for a fully personal, social and embodied existence in a quite different environment, an existence that would be causally connected to earthly life yet notably different – 'you do not sow the body that is to be, but a bare seed' (1 Corinthians 15.37). The body that is to be will be imperishable, not corruptible; glorious, not ugly; strong, not weak; and spiritual, not physical, in nature (1 Corinthians 15.42–44).

This life continues to be of great importance, as the place where every human pilgrimage begins, and where the seed of every human life is planted and nourished. But beyond this life, in a more glorious and imperishable world, each human pilgrimage will continue, learning to discard more of self and to learn more of God, and growing endlessly in that fullness of joy that the presence of God imparts. That is the Christian hope for the resurrection of the body – each person can pursue, in a life greater and wider than this, and in company with many beloved companions, an infinite journey into God.

45
The mythological worldview of the Bible

It is important to come to terms with the fact that the worldview of the Bible is very different from that of modern science and history. Christian faith began from a revolutionary disclosure of God in the life, death and resurrection of Jesus, from a life-transforming experience of the Spirit of God in the early Church, and from a new hope for immortality, for participation in the eternal life of God. But it was framed in terms of the worldview of the day. Lacking knowledge of the actual nature and history of the cosmos, that worldview was necessarily framed in poetic and imaginative terms, clothing spiritual insights in symbols and images that are not literally true.

The German New Testament scholar Rudolf Bultmann (1884–1976), in his lecture 'New Testament and Mythology', delivered in 1941, called this way of speaking 'mythology', meaning the presentation of spiritual truths as though they were factual and historical events. Modern Christians need to 'demythologize' such writings – that is, treat them as stories, uncover the spiritual truths they express, and show how they can be re-expressed in terms of modern knowledge.

The mythological view of the Bible is that the earth is a flat disc floating on water (the sea of chaos), while the sun, moon and stars are lamps hung on the dome of the sky. Heaven, where God and angels live, is above the sky, and the Underworld (Sheol, misleadingly called 'hell'), where the dead live, is below the ground.

About six thousand years ago, God created Adam, put him in a garden, and formed a woman out of one of his ribs. All present humans are descended from the eight people who were in Noah's Ark. Jesus' ancestry can be traced back to Noah over 67 generations (according to Luke; 53 generations, according to Matthew). With Jesus the history of the universe is about to come to an end.

It will end (or it should already have ended) like this. There will be great tribulations, plagues, wars and natural disasters. Then Jesus will return to earth with the angels and some of the resurrected dead and a number of the living chosen to rule with him, defeat Satan in a great battle at Armageddon and rule for a thousand years. After that there will be a universal resurrection of the dead, a judgement before a great white throne in which those whose names are in the book of life will be saved, and all others will be thrown into a lake of fire. Finally, sun, stars and sea will disappear, and a new city of Jerusalem will descend from the sky. The story of the earth, and indeed of the whole created universe, will be over.

Nobody who accepts the findings of modern science could think this was literally true, or even meant to be literally true. This account, largely taken from the early chapters of Genesis and the book of Revelation, is a visionary dream, to some extent a nightmare. It is vitally important for Christians to be clear that literal interpretations of this worldview must be decisively rejected. But why is it in the Bible, and what can we do with it today?

It is there because believers need to place the primal Christian elements of faith – the life of Jesus, the experience of the Spirit, and the hope for eternal fellowship with God – in a historical and cosmic context that brings out their true religious significance. The biblical writers did this as well as they could, but their imagined cosmic context was drastically mistaken. The Patristic theologians of the fourth and fifth centuries, and the Aristotelian theologians of the thirteenth century, did the same in different contexts, but they had little correct knowledge of the nature of the physical universe either. In our day, when we have much better, though still provisional, knowledge of the universe, we must do the same.

What happens when we do? All the physical details of the creation myth must be discarded, and the remaining poem should be read as expressing the truth that God is the only creator of the whole universe. In a similar way, all the physical details of the eschatological (end of the world) myth must be discarded. What the remaining poem expresses is that all forms of sin and oppression will be judged and destroyed; God's purpose will be realized; Christ, who is central to that purpose, will reign; and there will be a new creation, in which no evil or suffering will exist.

This will not, however, happen on this planet at some future time. As Jesus' resurrection was in another, 'spiritual' form of being, so the end of sin, the judgement on all human earthly actions, the realization of divine purpose, and the rule of Christ, will occur in a form of being beyond this space and time, in a new and incorruptible creation. Christ will not literally return to the planet earth. But the whole of human history will be taken into the life of God, and there sin will be destroyed, the divine goal for the life of the universe will be realized, and the whole universe will be renewed and completed in Christ.

That is what I think it means to say that 'Christ will come again to judge the living and the dead'. The cosmic Christ will be manifest and present in divine glory to all who have ever lived, to eliminate sin and suffering, and to bring all earthly lives that consent to his love to their perfection in conscious and transfiguring relation to God. These are the spiritual truths that are expressed by the mythological worldview of the Bible, a worldview that belongs to a cultural outlook we can no longer share.

46
The end of all things

Many classical Protestants believe that those who have died sleep until the day of resurrection, when all will rise from the dead for judgement, and be allocated to heaven, the presence and vision of God, or to hell, where they will suffer torment and final separation from God. Catholics and Orthodox Christians, however, generally think that at death those souls who have been made holy by the Spirit go to heaven, those who are unrepentantly evil go to hell, and those who are penitent and forgiven of mortal sin but are still imperfect enter an intermediate state, which Catholics call purgatory, where they can be purged of sin and prepare for heaven. At the Last Judgement all souls will be reunited with their bodies, and be finally assigned to heaven or hell.

If now we have a firmer grasp of the unlimited love of God shown in Jesus, if we accept that biblical teaching about final human destiny is phrased in non-literal symbolic terms and within a mythological worldview, and if we try to relate our beliefs as nearly as possible to the experienced resurrection of Jesus and the present experience of the Spirit, we might think rather differently and more charitably.

First, we will hope for resurrection in a spiritual, not an earthly realm ('flesh and blood cannot inherit the kingdom of God', 1 Corinthians 15.50). Second, we will not accept that a God of love will condemn anyone to endless torment in hell. Third, we might hope that all who do not fully, finally and consciously reject God will share for ever in the life of a new creation, filled with the presence and glory of God.

Hell – the rubbish heap, the outer darkness, the lake of fire – may indeed be a place where one becomes deeply conscious of the emptiness of a world without God, where one realizes that one has excluded oneself from the fellowship of love, and where one is tormented by the fires of selfish desire. It is a place where those who have rejected love experience what it is like to exist in a realm without love, where they have no power to escape the torment that follows from a world of hatred, greed and grasping desire, a torment they inflicted on others but themselves largely escaped on earth. The callous and violent will be judged, and the judgement will be that they should feel and know the harm they have inflicted on others. They will inhabit a self-created hell.

A God of justice will ensure that the unjust receive the punishment their acts deserve. Yet a God of love will ensure that such punishment is designed to lead to repentance and amendment of life, even if such repentance cannot be guaranteed. It is mean-minded to think that the door of repentance is closed at death for ever. The New Testament suggests that Jesus offered repentance to the dead after his resurrection, when he 'descended into hell': 'The gospel was proclaimed even to the dead, so that, though they had been judged in the flesh as everyone is judged, they might live in the spirit as God does' (1 Peter 4.6). These were not the righteous dead. On the contrary, they were those who had disobeyed God (1 Peter 3.18–20), whose 'every inclination of the thoughts of their hearts was only evil continually' (Genesis 6.5). This passage is, of course, part of the mythological worldview of the Bible, but its suggestion that even those who had been evil on earth might, after due punishment, repent and receive life in the Spirit is deeply congruent with the gospel of the unlimited love of God.

We might say that there is a door from hell to purgatory. Whether all will take it or not, we cannot tell. But the punishments of hell are partly designed to lead people to it, and perhaps God's purpose cannot be fully realized until everyone has either passed through it or finally ceased to be: 'As all die in Adam, so all will be made alive in Christ' (1 Corinthians 15.22). The purpose of God in Christ is that, as all die, so all should live in Christ. If some refuse this purpose, even the rather savagely retributive book of Revelation suggests that evil, and death and hell themselves, will be 'thrown into the lake of fire' (Revelation 20.14), where they will finally cease to be, and in the new heaven and earth 'nothing accursed will be found there any more' (Revelation 22.3).

In purgatory 'the fire' will test what sort of work each has done', and while there are rewards for some, in many cases 'the builder will be saved, but only as through fire' (1 Corinthians 3.13–15). Most of us will have much to learn, and much to unlearn, before we are ready for the vision of God and the fellowship with the saints who share in the divine life. In that place we may be sure that there will be many who never heard of Christ or who never joined any church during their lives, but who said 'yes' to a God who came secretly and unrecognized into their hearts, and who during their further pilgrimage learn who that God truly is. And there will be many who have suffered pain and anguish on earth, who find healing and ways in which to come to terms with their wounds, as they grow more fully into the wider communion of those who share the love of God.

It may well be, as the Orthodox and Catholic Churches teach, that there are souls already in heaven or Paradise, in the happiness of the clear vision of God. Jesus said to the penitent thief, 'Today you will be with me in Paradise' (Luke 23.43). Certainly, it seems right that we should pray for those who are continuing their journey beyond this life, and that we should ask for the prayers of those, the martyrs and saints, who have attained, or come nearer than us, to the vision of God in glory.

In the end, when the consequences of every earthly life have been worked out, when all that has to be learned from earthly life has been learned, when all earthly suffering has been healed, then Christ will hand over the kingdom to God the Father, 'so that God may be all in all' (1 Corinthians 15.20–28). Then we shall be resurrected in our final glorious form, and the whole creation shall be made new. For that state there is no literal description; the symbols of the Bible point toward the indescribable: 'There will be no more night; they need no light of lamp or sun, for the Lord God will be their light, and they will reign for ever and ever' (Revelation 22.5).

Prayer

47
Contemplation, devotion and discipline

In the end religious faith is not about intellectual belief. It is about prayer. What marks religion off from philosophy is that the religious believer prays, and does not simply have special beliefs about the nature of reality.

Prayer, of course, does presuppose some beliefs. Most basically, it presupposes that there is a supreme spiritual reality, a reality having the nature of consciousness. Further, that consciousness, knowing every possible state that could exist, actualizes and enjoys states of supreme beauty and goodness in itself. This consciousness of supreme intelligence, power, beauty, goodness and bliss is God.

Prayer is love of the good and the beautiful. To love something is to contemplate, pay attention to, appreciate and enjoy it. Part of prayer is to attend to and delight in all beautiful and good things – in music, the visual arts and literature, in friendship and shared activities, in the sciences and the pursuit of knowledge and understanding. But true prayer moves beyond all particular beautiful things, to contemplate and admire that which is the source of all beauty and is itself supremely beautiful, the being of God.

All instances of beauty and goodness in the world can be used as steps to ascend towards absolute beauty. Prayer is a discipline of the mind that leads from the finite image to the infinite source of its being, that sees the infinite in the finite. What we see in part and in multiple images can lead beyond itself to something not further away, but deeper within. There at the centre of each being, the source of its life, is that which can no longer be named, because it transcends the limitations of human thought. All we can see is the direction in which the mind must move towards a dazzling light that illuminates all things yet, like the sun, cannot itself be directly scrutinized by normal sight.

Prayer is a preparation for the vision of uncreated light. Yet we should not be discouraged if such a goal seems at present beyond us. All that is needed is that we see the light reflected in the everyday things of our world. That is, we see each good and beautiful thing as pointing beyond itself, or drawing us within itself, to that which is manifest yet never wholly expressed. That sense of transcendence, of something beyond and greater and yet present and manifest, is the sense of God.

There are many paths of prayer that have been important in the Christian tradition, each of which expresses in a different way the love of the good and beautiful that is the heart of prayer. For some, when the thoughts of the mind are quietened, and feelings are calmed, and words are left behind, the silent music of the presence of God will flood the whole world with light. This prayer requires making time for quiet meditation, for stilling the mind. Many find it helpful just to sit, with back straight and head upright, breathing regularly and calmly, and to repeat a short phrase to help concentrate the mind, like some form of the Eastern Orthodox 'Jesus prayer' such as 'Lord Jesus, Son of God, have mercy'. A short biblical phrase might be personally chosen and adapted, like 'Christ in me, the hope of glory'. The purpose is just to prevent all sorts of other thoughts disturbing concentration. Words are not really necessary. Some may find that concentrating on an object like a candle or an icon is helpful. Others may prefer simply to sit in silence, with eyes closed. But verbal thoughts or reflections should be avoided in this sort of prayer. The point is simply to be open to the presence of God, and become aware of that personal ground of being which is never absent, though often hidden and unrecognized. Most practitioners find that a regular daily period of between ten and twenty minutes is best for such a practice. This is the prayer of quiet, of contemplation.

For others, at least for those who are Christians, meditation on the person of Jesus will disclose God in peculiarly personal ways. We may read a Gospel passage – just a few verses – about an incident in Jesus' life, or one of Jesus' sayings. We may call up in our imagination the thought of Jesus acting upon or near to us or speaking directly to us, and then we can come to see God's beauty, wisdom and healing power in him. As we acknowledge him as the one who manifests God to us, love and reverence is aroused in the heart, and this too is love for the good and the beautiful, manifest in the presence of Jesus. That is how Christians can worship Jesus, because in him the perfect beauty of God is manifested for us in a human life. For Christians, he is the way by which we come closer to God, and our love for him is true prayer, the openness of the mind and heart to the creator of all worlds. This is a short form of the sort of prayer found in the spiritual exercises of Ignatius Loyola (1491–1556). Each Gospel meditation might begin with a prayer that God might through it reveal the divine nature or purpose more fully, and end with a resolution to perform one specific action during the day that has been suggested by this inner encounter with Christ. This is the prayer of devotion and of intimate love.

There is another path of prayer. For some the path to knowledge of supreme goodness is by way of a personal commitment of the will, a self-imposed discipline or practice. The discipline of reciting the Psalms in turn, a few at a time, that takes place in the daily liturgy, faithful attendance at a worship service or at the Eucharist, daily Bible reading, and a commitment to small acts of self-denial, like temporarily renouncing some foods or liquids, or performing secret acts of charity and kindness to others – this too is prayer. This path does not focus on experiences or emotions. Nor should it ever be seen as some sort of attempt to force God to be impressed by our efforts. It is rather a practical commitment that will train the mind in faithfulness and charity both to God and to others. Such acts are performed simply to honour God, for the sake of God alone.

Without asking for any particular reward, we might undertake such disciplines just because we thereby commit ourselves to being open and responsive to God. This is our declared love of God in action, in particular acts that take time and effort, and prepare us to be better servants of God.

Sometimes people express a wish that they had more faith – meaning that God would make them believe more easily or feel more intensely. But one thing we can always do is commit ourselves to the best we know. The practice itself will prepare us for union with God. Of course such prayers must not be 'vain repetitions', meant to accrue merit for ourselves, or gabbled meaninglessly. Yet there is a place for disciplined practice. We do not always have to be looking for intense emotions or feelings of inner sincerity or significance. We can just undertake the practice, doing it because we intend to honour and commit our lives to God. In some ways it may even be better if we do not feel like doing it, or if our feelings are not engaged. For moods change and are not wholly under our control. But we can set ourselves to do these tasks, and over time – perhaps over quite a long time – our actions will shape our thoughts and feelings and, more importantly, our lives. This is the prayer of discipline. It too expresses love of the good and the beautiful, a practical and effective love that puts our lives at the disposal of the God who is perfect love.

48
The prayer of reception

A fourth path is that of placing ourselves at the disposal of the Spirit of God, who filled the life of Jesus and is sent to lead us into the truth, the unveiled reality of the life of God. The fruits of the Spirit are the beautiful characteristics that the Spirit produces in the lives of men and women, insofar as they are open to the action of the Spirit. These characteristics are set out in Galatians 5.22, and meditation on that short text can be used as a guide to the characteristics Christians should seek to cultivate in themselves. There are of course many other biblical passages that could be used in a similar way – the Beatitudes, in Matthew 5.1–12, and passages like Ephesians 4.22–32, are very helpful. But I will use the Galatians verse as an outline of the characteristics the Spirit can and will produce in human lives.

First is love – which involves both delight in the joys of others and compassion for their sorrows. We should pray that we find real happiness in the happiness of others. There should be no envy or resentment, but a concern that they should find deep and lasting happiness, and joy when they do. We should pray that we may always seek to alleviate the sufferings of others, never seeking to harm others, even when they seek to harm us, but always being concerned for their good. Such love should be without limits, given to all beings capable of happiness and sorrow without exception. To know the Spirit is to be changed by the Spirit, to become like the Spirit, so far as that is possible. In this respect, prayer is the conformity of the mind and heart to God, allowing ourselves to become like that which we revere.

Such prayer seeks first to change ourselves, but to ensure that such a change will affect our conduct towards others. It is prayer, not just self-help, because it seeks to be receptive to the Spirit of love that was in Jesus. Love requires the capacity to receive as well as the capacity to give, and our love for God needs to include our reception of God's love, to let it live in us as an inward and transforming power. In such prayer we should take time to consider what things in our own lives give us the opportunity to rejoice with others or to show compassion. We should try to feel the joys and sorrows that others feel, and to understand why they feel as they do. We should imagine specific things that we can do to help, and we should think of ourselves as empowered by the divine Spirit, which can raise us above our own limited and self-centred desires. It is in such prayer that the Spirit may more effectively work in and through us.

The second fruit of the Spirit is joy. Life lived in the conscious presence of God cannot be defeated by despair. To have a joyful mind is always to think of things that will make human lives more beautiful, and to be thankful for all good things, however small.

The third fruit of the Spirit is peace. True peace is harmony and reconciliation, a sharing of experience and co-operation in bringing about good things. It is also the cultivation of a mind not distressed by anger or given to destructiveness. To be at peace is to be calm in all circumstances, because we know we are grounded in God, who cannot be injured or destroyed by anything at all.

The fourth fruit is patience. This is the capacity not to insist upon things happening just when and as we wish. We must act as well as we can and leave the outcome to God, not despairing if things do not go as we plan, and never thinking that our actions have been useless. Action without attachment is the patience that the Spirit can instil.

The fifth fruit is kindness. We should have an attitude of universal loving-kindness. Kindness is not doing what our duty demands. It is going beyond duty, and helping others, often secretly, to achieve what is good and to realize their own potential.

The sixth fruit is generosity. We possess nothing that God does not freely give, and insofar as God lives and acts in us, we will in turn give freely. The opposite of generosity is possessiveness, the desire to own and control and exclude others. The generous person will know that things are not to be possessed, but to be used for the sake of good.

The seventh fruit is faithfulness. Trust builds up human relationships. Fidelity enables us to rely on others, and lets them know that we will not fail them. God asks us for total commitment, and our human relationships should be such that friendships will not be broken by arguments or irritations. Whatever happens, we shall show faithfulness to our promises and to our friends.

The eighth fruit is gentleness. The Christian way is not one of power and conquest, but of gentleness and sensitivity to others. Gentleness consists in being mindful of the feelings of others, and in not forcing them to bow to our wishes.

The ninth fruit is self-control. Always to be in control of our desires, never to be distracted by selfish passion, but always bearing in mind our chosen goal – that is a characteristic important to a Christian life.

In outlining the fruits of the Spirit, I have wholly ignored the complexities that inevitably arise in real life – dilemmas about when we should forgive, when we must exercise compulsion to avoid greater harm to others, or when we cannot be kind. The Christian life is not one that ignores the realities of evil and conflict in society. Thus meditation on these fruits must always be individual and particular, and it cannot be encompassed in any brief and general list like the one I have just provided. It must be a self-examination of a unique life and situation in the presence of the Spirit of Jesus Christ. This is a difficult discipline, but it is vital that these ideals are contemplated, that we attempt to conform our lives to them as far as possible, and that we ask for the power of the Spirit to enable us to do so. This is the prayer of reception, of receptivity to the Spirit of God. It could be called 'confession', since it involves self-examination. Yet it does not concentrate on our sins and failures. It rather concentrates on the positive characteristics the Spirit wills to give to us, and on the possibility that we may become instruments of the Spirit of God, in a real if always imperfect way.

49

Intercession

Some think that asking God for things is the heart of prayer. Others cannot see the point of asking God for anything, since God knows all things anyway, and must already be acting for the best. But if prayer is love of God, then our desire will be that God is more fully known by us, and that God will act in the world through us. 'Asking' is simply being open to God's presence and power. God gives, but we must be open to receive. Intercession is learning to be truly receptive to God, so that we may be channels of God's compassion and concern.

God has placed us in a community of persons, in which all give to and receive from each other. We can help others physically: God gives us that possibility and responsibility. So we may help others spiritually, for thought is an effective power. Intercession opens the world to the action of God. It is not that God would not otherwise act. But God would not act in this way, through the openness of our minds in their concern for others.

The created cosmos operates in accordance with elegant and universal laws, and its elements are interconnected in such a way that each event reverberates to some extent on all others. The laws of nature do not form a closed, predetermined causal web, and many sorts of influence, including the influence of God, can be real causal factors on how the future unfolds. Yet such influences do not exist in isolation, and the difference they make to the universe is often too complex for human calculation. So when we ask God to do something, there may be many factors of which we are unaware. Nature is flexible, but its causal laws cannot be continually suspended by miracles, or natural laws would not exist. So the existence of the laws of nature that God has created will limit the sorts of things that God might do in answer to prayer.

In addition, God gives humans freedom, and often they choose the path of selfish desire, hatred and greed. This path obstructs and seeks to exclude the influence of God. We cannot know how far our requests are blocked by the resistance of human wills.

Nevertheless if there is a supreme spiritual source of all reality, and if all free finite acts are known and responded to by God, then our acts of intercession, of holding the needs of others in the presence of God and asking that they be met, will elicit a response in God. That response may not take the precise form we wish, but it will positively affect the future for good.

To pray for others is to think of their needs, and to ask for their freedom from all that hurts and harms them. If our prayer is serious, it will involve some appropriate action on our part, however limited. But it will also contribute some influence of its own to the causal nexus, guided by God, that forges the future. In that way, prayer will 'work' – not in predictable or measurable ways, but as an influence on the mind of God, who will use it in ways unknowable by us to guide the temporal process. It opens a space in the world for the healing influence of God.

There are many forms of intercession. One is to envisage the person or situation prayed for in as much detail as possible, thinking of those things that could be helped by the healing power of God. Then think of them surrounded by the presence and power of God, and being upheld by the divine life. Finally, determine what you can do personally to help in this or in some similar case nearer to hand. That is intercession – imaginatively placing persons and situations in the presence of God for healing. It is a natural part of our dependence on God.

Such dependence begins with ourselves. Intercession properly includes prayer for ourselves, that we may discover our own unique possibilities, and be able to use them fruitfully in the service of others. So each morning we might think of the possibilities and opportunities that lie before us. Each day we might aim, in the words of Mother Teresa, to do something beautiful for God. And each day, at its end, we might think of all the good things we have seen and done, and give thanks for the particular gifts of being that we have received.

Sometimes our own lives may be darkened by suffering, by pain, by distress or loss. Such times must come, and then our prayer must be to endure, perhaps to cry in anguish or even anger and frustration. The Psalms show us that the expression of bewilderment or anger is sometimes necessary for us, as we seek to come to terms with the suffering of a world estranged from God. God does not will us to suffer evil, as some sort of personal punishment. Some arises from the necessities of nature, which alone enable us to have life. Much is caused by the hatred and selfish desire of others. Some may be the consequence of past acts of our own. What matters is that in the end we might find ourselves able to offer our suffering to God. The death of self, of our hopes, of all we are attached to and have desired, can become a sharing in the death of Christ, offered for the healing of the world. With him in Gethsemane we may pray, 'Father, if you are willing, remove this cup from me; yet, not my will but yours be done' (Luke 22.42).

What God wills is that all the wounds of life shall be healed, and that we should share in eternal life. Healing can be slow and difficult. It involves acknowledging that painful experiences have shaped what we are, in ways we would not have wished. Yet with the help of God we can endure, overcome resentment and disappointment, and find a

positive path of self-surrender to God, and a positive hope of fuller life
in God. That is our prayer for ourselves, as it is our prayer for all who
are in trouble or distress. It acknowledges the dependence of imperfect
and often suffering beings on a God of supreme beauty and bliss, whose
will is that we shall finally be liberated from evil and share in the divine
nature. This is the prayer of intercession, of our absolute dependence
upon God.

50
Prayer as communion of being

It is important that there should be special times set aside for prayers
of contemplation, devotion, discipline, reception and intercession. But
the ideal for Christian life is that the whole of life should be prayer. It
should be prayer in the sense of being in communion with God. The
Christian life is not being heroically alone in an indifferent universe.
It is being in conscious and continual relationship to that supreme
wisdom and bliss, creativity and compassion, that is God. Nor is this an
external relationship, as if God were another distinct and finite person
with whom you could converse. It is deeper than that. It is a relationship of union, but a union in which the individual self is not
extinguished or dissolved.

In John's Gospel, Jesus prays to the Father that his disciples 'may be
one, as we are one' (John 17.11). The nature of this unity is further
expounded in this way: 'as you, Father, are in me and I am in you, may
they also be in us' (John 17.21). It is not a unity that extinguishes difference and individuality. It is a unity of coinherence. The Father is 'in'
Christ, Christ is 'in' the Father, the disciples are 'in' Christ, and Christ
is 'in' the disciples.

The ultimate teaching of Christianity is non-duality, the coinherence
of all things in God. The ultimate prayer is the realization of non-
duality, the knowledge and sense that individual life is set wholly within God and suffused wholly by God.

The individual self is not and will never be divine, in the sense of
being omniscient and omnipotent. But each self is centred in God,
and God is the true centre of each self. Divinity is not set far away,
above the heavens or beyond the sea. It is within us, as our limited and
egoistic desires expand to embrace all things. We are within it, as the
unlimited ocean of being within which we play out our finite lives. The
divine life lives in and through us, as we express one small finite part
of the infinite life of God, and as our minds and hearts open out to
apprehend and feel the unlimited riches of the being of God.

The sense of God is not the sense of being in the presence of an invisible person. It is the sense that the reality within which we exist is not the world of distinct material objects it often seems to be. It is a reality of Spirit, of awareness, intelligence, wisdom and bliss, sometimes hidden but often expressed in the finite forms of our space and time. It is in God that 'we live and move and have our being' (Acts 17.28). Moreover, this reality is the innermost power that seeks expression in our daily lives, as the divine creativity and compassion finds finite form in us. The author of Ephesians prays 'that Christ may dwell in your hearts' (Ephesians 3.17), and this indwelling Christ works through 'the new self, created according to the likeness of God' (Ephesians 4.24).

The life of prayer is the whole of life lived with the sense of being parts of one infinite spiritual reality of wisdom and bliss, parts whose calling is to manifest in a unique and individual way the nature of the divine Spirit that is the centre of each being, as the root of its existence. This is the 'sharing in the divine nature' of which 2 Peter speaks (1.4).

To realize such a life we need to be liberated from the world that is corrupted by egoistic desires. This means a discipline of detachment from such desires, and a constantly renewed faith (trust) in the divine power of wisdom and compassion that was authentically manifested in the person of Jesus. Irreligion is life without that discipline and faith, life centred on the egoistic self, which seeks to possess all things and preserve itself at all costs. True religion is life as prayer, life centred on the divine Self, which seeks to share all things and surrender the subjective self to divine goodness and beauty in all its forms. In such surrender the self is fulfilled, for then it expands to become one with the Self of all. Then, as Paul writes, 'I have been crucified with Christ; and it is no longer I who live, but it is Christ who lives in me' (Galatians 2.20). This is the prayer of communion, of the unity of all things in Christ, and in its perfect form it seems to me to be the final goal of Christian living.

Further reading

The creation

1 The beginning

There are many good books by scientists on the origin of the universe, from a Christian perspective. Arthur Peacocke and John Polkinghorne in particular are helpful. I recommend Polkinghorne's *Science and Creation* (SPCK, 1988) and Peacocke's *Paths from Science Towards God* (Oneworld Publications, 2001). My own contribution is *Pascal's Fire* (Oneworld Publications, 2006). *Religion and Science* by Ian Barbour (SCM Press, 1998) remains the classic text in the field.

2 The wisdom of creation

On the evolution of life, Simon Conway Morris's *Life's Solution* (Cambridge University Press, 2003) shows how Christians can see evolution as a purposive process aimed at producing intelligent life.

4 The image of God

My *Religion and Human Nature* (Oxford University Press, 1998), chap. 7, deals with the evolution and nature of the human soul.

5 The Fall

Religion and Human Nature, chap. 8, gives a fuller account of original sin, partly based on the pioneering work of F. R. Tennant, *Philosophical Theology* (Cambridge University Press, 1930).

The Hebrew Bible

6 The birth of monotheism

Very little is known with certainty about the origins of religion. A good introduction is A. Evans-Pritchard, *Theories of Primitive Religion* (Clarendon Press, 1965). My *The Case for Religion*, chaps 1 and 2 (Oneworld Publications, 2004), deals with the topic.

Among many good books on scholarly views of the Hebrew Bible, I recommend Bernhard Anderson, *The Living World of the Old Testament* (4th edn, Longman, 1988).

Jesus in the Gospels

11 The kingdom

There are many excellent commentaries on the Gospels. In general, one text that presents the best modern scholarship, with contributors from every main Christian church, is *The Oxford Commentary on the Bible*, edited by John Barton and John Muddiman (Oxford University Press, 2001). A good, short, representative book on scholarly views of Jesus is Martin Forward, *Jesus: A Short Biography* (Oneworld Publications, 1998).

12 The infancy narratives

A book that presents two contrasting views of Jesus, one more conservative, one more radical, is Marcus Borg and N. T. Wright, *The Meaning of Jesus* (HarperCollins, 1999).

18 Apocalypse

A good account of the way biblical language is richly metaphorical and allusive is given by George Caird in *The Language and Imagery of the Bible* (Duckworth, 1980).

The early development of doctrine

24 Incarnation

One good account of the development of Christian doctrines in the early Church is Frances Young, *From Nicaea to Chalcedon* (SCM Press, 1983). An earlier, classic account is J. N. D. Kelly, *Early Christian Doctrines* (A. & C. Black, 1958). My own account of incarnation is given in *Religion and Revelation*, part 4, sect. D (Oxford University Press, 1994), and in *Re-thinking Christianity*, chap. 4 (Oneworld Publications, 2007).

25 The Trinity

I give fuller accounts of the Trinity in *Religion and Creation*, chap. 13 (Oxford University Press, 1996), and *Re-thinking Christianity*, chap. 5.

26 Atonement

I consider the doctrine of the atonement in *Religion and Human Nature*, chap. 9 (Oxford University Press, 1998), and *Re-thinking Christianity*, chap. 6.

27 The Church

I consider the doctrine of the Church in *Religion and Community*, parts 2 and 3 (Oxford University Press, 2000), and *Re-thinking Christianity*, chap. 12.

Christianity in relation to the non-Christian world

28 Humanist values

I give a fuller treatment of humanism and religion in *Religion and Community*, chap. 5 (Oxford University Press, 2000).

29 Indian religious traditions

Among many excellent books on the relation between Indian religious traditions and Christianity, I have found particularly helpful the work of Bede Griffiths, for example in *The Marriage of East and West* (Collins, 1982). My own views can be found in *Concepts of God* (Oneworld Publications, 1998). For a further treatment of East Asian and Muslim views in relation to Christianity, see my *Religion and Revelation*, part 3 (Oxford University Press, 1994), and also *Religion and Community*, chaps 1–4.

Defining moments in Christian history

32 Martyrs, icons and monks

The subject matter of sections 32–5 are more fully treated in *Re-thinking Christianity* (Oneworld Publications, 2007). An excellent little book on the history of Christian doctrine is *Christianity: Two Thousand Years*, edited by Richard Harries and Henry Mayr-Harting (Oxford University Press, 2001).

36 The Bible in a critical age

I have written about the interpretation of the Bible in *What the Bible Really Teaches* (SPCK, 2004). The impact of modern science on religious belief is discussed in my *Pascal's Fire* (Oneworld Publications, 2006).

37 The new perspective of science

The impact of modern science on religious belief is discussed in my *Pascal's Fire*.

39 Morality and purpose

One rather tentative exposition of natural law by Thomas Aquinas can be found in *Summa Theologiae*, 1a2ae, questions 93 and 94.

41 The twentieth century

Karl Barth's major work is the multi-volumed *Church Dogmatics* (T. & T. Clark, 1936–69). But *The Epistle to the Romans* (Oxford University Press, 1933) is an important early work that gives a good flavour of his approach.

Paul Tillich, *Systematic Theology* (Nisbet, 1953) and John Macquarrie, *Principles of Christian Theology* (SCM Press, 1966) are important books.

A useful book by Karl Rahner is *Foundations of Christian Faith* (Crossroad, 1997).

On liberation theology, see Jürgen Moltmann, *Theology of Hope* (SCM Press, 1967) and Gustavo Gutiérrez, *A Theology of Liberation* (SCM Press, 1974).

The final goal of creation

43 The future

One possible future for the Christian Church is discussed in my *Religion and Community*, part 2 (Oxford University Press, 2000).

44 The resurrection of the dead

The questions of the ultimate end of the universe and the resurrection are considered in more detail in my *Pascal's Fire* (Oneworld Publications, 2006).

45 The mythological worldview of the Bible

The key text for reflection on the mythological worldview of the Bible is Rudolf Bultmann, *Jesus Christ and Mythology* (T. & T. Clark, 1958).

46 The end of all things

The Roman Catholic theologian Karl Rahner provides an excellent example of a reconsideration of traditional Christian thinking about life after death in *Foundations of Christian Faith*, chap. 9 (Crossroad, 1997).